THE TIME MIRACLE

A Practical Guide for Slowing Down, Rethinking
Time, and Designing a Meaningful Life

THE TIME MIRACLE

A Practical Guide for Slowing Down, Rethinking
Time, and Designing a Meaningful Life

JEAN PAUL ZOGBY

Time Lighthouse Publishing,
London, New York, Dubai

ISBN 978-0-9957347-1-5

Time Lighthouse Publishing
Southwell Gardens, London, U.K.

Printed in the United Kingdom. First Printing, 2018

For information about special discounts available for bulk purchases, sales promotions, fund-raising, and educational needs, contact Jean Paul Zogby at jp@jpzogby.com

Important Notice to Readers - Your <u>FREE</u> Gifts

As a way of saying thanks for your purchase, I am offering **FREE** instant access to the **Online Speed of Time Test**

<u>Click Here to measure how fast time runs in your mind</u>!

By taking this short online test, you will receive a **<u>detailed report</u>** on your personality and how that affects your Speed of Time.

Available for ~~$7.99~~ <u>FREE</u> for a limited time only

Building a relationship with my readers is the greatest thing about writing. By joining my mailing list, you will receive:

- **Free** Self-improvement Courses

- **The Ultimate Healthy Brain Diet**

- Monthly newsletter on the latest brain research

- Special Offers & Updates on new book releases

To download a **<u>FREE</u>** copy of the *Ultimate Guide to a Healthy Brain Diet*, please visit the author's website at <u>http://www.jpzogby.com</u>

OR

<u>Click here to download a **Free** copy of the Ultimate Guide to a Healthy Brain Diet</u>

To Mom, for all your sacrifices and infinite love.

To Dad, for making me who I am. How I wish you were here.

To my wife and love of my life, Roula, I am so lucky to share my life and love with you.

To my children Stephanie, Chloe, and Anthony, you provide me with a constant source of joy and pride.
You will inherit the world and make it a much better place.

Table of Contents

Preface

In my early twenties, I got a wake-up call: my father passed away after a long fight with cancer. With a family history of cancer also affecting all my uncles and grandfathers, I thought, *it's only a matter of time before it's my turn.*

I was all the more mindful of this having brushes with—but surviving—almost certain death on four different occasions while growing up during the sixteen-year Lebanese Civil War.

Yes, I was among the fortunate. But I also had experienced the horror of seeing some of my closest friends perish.

I guess these experiences are the subconscious reason behind my obsession with time—and my urge to make the most of it.

Medical science advancements have been increasing man's life expectancy. The average human life span of our ancestor cavemen was just twenty years. Currently man's life expectancy is at seventy-six years—and projected to reach 150 by the year 2100!

Obviously, I cannot live that long so I won't enjoy that much more time here on this Earth. But I wanted to slow down time and prolong the shorter life all of us are living now. So after spending 6 years interviewing neuroscientists and researching the latest scientific findings in the fields of neuroscience and psychology to understand how we perceive time and what we can do to slow it down, I wrote my first book, *The Power of Time Perception.*

For this book, *The Time Miracle*, I wanted to break down the time that's available to us into typical usages during our lifespan. I wanted to see how we are using it, analyze where we are wasting it, and ultimately figure out how we *should be* using it. Then we can make the most of our time and experience greater happiness, meaning, and longevity.

To that end, I've divided this book into four sections.

- **Part One, The Lottery of Life**, examines the value time holds for us and how we use it in general.
- **Part Two, Squeeze More Out of Life!**, explores time usage, and presents simple but effective "hacks" to optimize our sleep time, eating time, money-earning time, and time spent on media.
- **Part Three, Happiness & Meaning**, explores one of the main factors that contributes to our happiness and the path to achieving meaning in life.
- **Part Four, Stretching Your Life Essence Years**, offers practical ways for slowing down our experience of time and making the most of it so that we experience perceived longevity and a fulfilling life.

It is natural to feel threatened by, or helpless towards, things we do not understand or cannot control. However, if we understand the miracle of time and learn how to use it wisely, it will no longer be our enemy.

My hope is that by reading this book, you'll be able to analyze the way you likely spend your time, get a feel for how best to optimize that, and "stretch" your available time into a happier, more meaningful life for you.

PART ONE

THE LOTTERY OF LIFE

1

You Made It!

Your Lucky Ticket

❧

"One life—a little gleam of Time between two Eternities. No
second chance to us for evermore."
– Thomas Carlyle

Welcome to the Universe! It is truly a miracle that you are here.
Having slept for a few million years, you finally made it! The
odds that you are alive at this moment in time are one in 400 quadrillion;
do you want to know why?

Well, a ridiculously lengthy list of highly improbable events all had to
happen for you to be here. If any single one of them had not happened,
you would not be sitting reading this book right now.

It's as if the whole Universe has conspired to bring you here—and it
all started millions of years ago.

Standing Tall

About 50 million years ago, the tectonic plate that carries India (it was
an island at that time) started pushing into the main Asian continent at
the rate of approximately 30 cm each year. Over several million years, this

slowly forced the Himalayan mountain range to rise steadily, diverting wind currents and significantly altering weather patterns across the planet.

Thousands of miles away, in East Africa, the change in global climate triggered dry weather and droughts that gradually transformed the dense forests into ever-expanding grasslands. There, in those jungles, lived a bunch of apes.

Researchers believe our ancestors (those apes) were forced to stray away from the trees into those open fields, where they were exposed to predators, such as lions and tigers, from whom they had previously been safe. The new conditions pushed our ancestors to start walking on their hind legs; that adaptation allowed them to see above the grass line and detect approaching danger. It also freed their hands to pick tools such as sticks, bones, or stones, for use as hunting weapons or for cracking nuts. And that, my friends, was the start of the age of technology.

At this stage, the human brain began to develop rapidly in size, which ultimately led to the emergence of intelligence.

Now, if India did not crash into Asia, we would have never left those trees. Fortunately, the trees left us and after a long sequence of highly unlikely events, mankind embarked on an impressive evolutionary journey.

Still Here!

Now, move forward in time to 70,000 B.C.

A super-volcano called Toba, on Sumatra in Indonesia, went off, blowing roughly 650 miles of vaporized rock into the air. The eruption rained a thick ash layer that covered the Indian Ocean, the Arabian and South China Seas, and the whole of South Asia, destroying acres and acres of plants and vegetation.

With so much ash and dust in the air, the sun was dimmed for six years, dropping temperatures on Earth by as much as twenty degrees and resulting in another global climate change. Starvation and the noxious gases in the atmosphere reduced the entire human population to just about a thousand people. One study says it even hit a low of forty people[1]. You can say we almost vanished.

Fortunately we made it back, although it took us almost 200,000 years to repopulate and reach our first billion. This goes to show you how lucky we are to be still here.

Now, what I have cited is just one catastrophic event out of hundreds more that affected the whole human race across the centuries and millennia. But we made it and somehow managed to survive each and every considerable challenge thrown at us. There were also challenges that had to be overcome for *you*—yes, you in particular—to exist.

Nothing Short of a Miracle

According to statistical gurus, the probability that your parents met the way they did and ended up having a relationship that lasted long enough to result in an offspring is around one in 40 million. Factor in the fact that you are the unique result of the fusion of one specific egg out of ten thousand eggs with one specific sperm out of 12 trillion sperm. The probability for that one particular sperm, with half your name written on it, to triumphantly hit that one particular egg, with the other half of your name, is one in 400 quadrillion.

The fact that you are here also presupposes that every one of your ancestors, going all the way back to the dawn of life, lived to reproductive age and produced that unbroken lineage leading up to you. If we consider only Homo sapiens, that's going to be around 150,000 generations. The right sperm had to meet the right egg in each one of those generations to create your grandparents, your grandparent's parents, your great-great-great grandparents, and so on. If at any point in time the wrong sperm met the wrong egg, the offspring, although being similar to you in some ways, would not *be* really you. The result would probably have looked like your cousin Eugene—who you never really liked anyway!

Evolutionary biologist and author Richard Dawkins puts it nicely in *Unweaving the Rainbow:*

> We are going to die, and that makes us the lucky ones. Most people are never going to die because they are never going to be born. The potential people who could have been here in my place but who will in fact never see the light of day outnumber the sand grains of Arabia… In the teeth of these stupefying odds, it is you and I, in our ordinariness that are here.

The probability for that extremely unlikely and utterly indisputable chain of events to occur is the same as consecutively winning the Powerball jackpot lottery every day for the next 50,000 years. That is, by definition, what we call a miracle: an event that is so unlikely as to be almost impossible!

You Got the Lucky Ticket!

Now, I have just showed you that you are nothing short of a miracle. You beat all odds, you won the "lottery of life," and you performed a miracle by just being born. So, congrats!

But what *is* your prize? How much did you actually win? How valuable is it?

And more importantly—how do you plan to spend your winnings?

As you read this book, you will note a "*Time Miracle Task*" at the end of each chapter with clear action points. I suggest you grab a notebook and complete these tasks so the book ideas relate to your own personal experience.

Time Miracle Task

Do you have enough time to do all the things you want to?
_____Yes _____ No

What would you do if you could free up more time?

_____

_____

_____

_____

2

Your Life Winnings

Time - The Ultimate Prize

∽∾

"Teach us to number our days so that we may gain
a heart of wisdom."
– Psalm 90

Time Winnings

By winning the lottery of life, you won the most valuable prize of all: time. The value your prize holds consists of a priceless number of hours, minutes, and seconds that you are given to exist. Those add up to a period of time that is kept hidden from you—and you must spend this amount *without knowing when it will run out.*

It's like constantly spending from a specific credit card without knowing the remaining balance. The day will certainly come when the limit is reached. You won't be able to make any more purchases. It's the same with your limited time on Earth.

Our days are numbered. As of 2017, the average life expectancy in the U.S. is approximately 78 years. It is around 82 years in Canada, 80 years in Europe, and close to 90 years in Japan and South Korea.

But not all these years in your life are equally valuable. The first four years of your life essentially do not really exist for you, in terms of your consciousness. You barely have any recollection of what happened, and if it wasn't for a couple of fleeting childhood memories, it is almost as if you were not there!

Then come your teenage years; here, didn't that time run so slowly for you, as you were so incredibly eager to grow up?

This phase is followed by your adult years. That's really when time started to speed up for you and become more valuable to you.

The upshot is, time increases in value for each and every one of us as it gets consumed and depleted.

Your Payout

Let's put this insight aside for a moment. We are going to regard each year of our time here as having the same value for us so we can estimate the value of the "lottery prize" you won and thus determine how efficient you are at using that prize.

We will use the U.S. life expectancy as our basis and view the prize time as being seventy-eight years.

Or, 912 months.

Or, 27,759 days.

Or, just 666,216 hours!

In order to enjoy our life prize to the utmost and subsequently have "the time of our life," we need to plan what are we going to do with the years, days, hours, and minutes at our disposal.

If we fail to divide our time up into the various "tasks at hand," that time will just slip away. With "unplanned living,"—i.e., when we don't think about how we should spend our time—we overlook many golden opportunities there for us.

To start, let's break down how the "average person" will typically spend their time (even if *you're* not average). We'll split the time into three time-spending categories:

- **Time spent on basic needs.** This includes sleeping, eating, personal hygiene; essentially anything a person needs to do to survive. Time invested in this category generates **health.**

- **Time spent earning money.** This includes the education needed to obtain and start a career, the actual working hours, and any time spent driving or commuting to work. These are all the things a person has to do to earn money and support their lifestyle. Time invested in this category generates **money** (mainly) in some form or another.

- **The remaining time available for a person to "enjoy" life.** This is a person's leisure time—the free time someone has to do hobbies, enjoy friendships, get entertained, and have fun. Time invested in this category mainly generates **memorable moments** that make up a person's life story.

These categories are not mutually exclusive. For instance, you could be someone who enjoys their work and derives satisfaction from what they do. In this case, the time you spend earning money would overlap with the time you spend enjoying life. Still, through coming to understand the amount of time you (uh, the average person) spend on these various time categories, you will better appreciate how valuable your time on Earth truly is. When your day-to-day activities are summed up over the course of a lifetime, you may well be shocked to discover how much of your life goes into performing *insignificant* daily tasks and how little time you have available for the things that matter most.

We're going to base our understanding on the findings of The American Time Use Survey (ATUS). It's a study released annually by the United States Census Bureau and sponsored by the Bureau of Labor Statistics (BLS).

The survey measures how people spend their time on various activities, such as working, leisure, childcare, and household activities. What follows is a brief summary of the results from the 2016 ATUS, combined with the findings of a few other similar studies, for how a typical American spends their time on average. (As it turns out, it's not much different for how people in the rest of the world spend their time.)

Time Spent on Basic Needs—Generating Health

Sleeping

You'll spend around twenty-nine years sleeping! The 2016 annual ATUS showed that people sleep for 8 hours and 50 minutes a day—thirteen minutes more than what was reported a decade ago.

If you average only eight hours of sleep a night, i.e., one third of a day, that means you're going to sleep for one-third of your life! If you live to the age of 78, you would have spent 26 years tucked in bed. This is assuming that you don't nap during the day as well.

Out of those 26 years, Canadian health experts estimate that people will experience seven years of insomnia. Yes, that is how long you'll spend lying awake at night waiting for Mr. Sandman!

Of course, sleep is essential for life, and you cannot get by without it. But that's a big chunk of your precious time that you could've spent doing so many other things.

While sleeping, you lose awareness of your senses. You'll have around four to six dreams on average each night, or approximately 2,000 dreams a year—although you'll forget 80 percent of them. If it wasn't for those few remembered dreams, the years you'll spend sleeping are barely an aspect of your conscious life. When you wake up, you usually have no recollection of what it was like to be asleep. It is as if you stopped existing while sleeping!

These 26 years of sleeping leave you with approximately 52 years to live and enjoy your life!

Eating

You'll spend 3.5 years of your life eating. The ATUS study showed that an average American spends 67 minutes eating and drinking each day. This adds up to a staggering 30,600 hours of eating in a lifetime. Incidentally, the total amount of food you will consume during that time is close to 80 tons!

Many people organize their life around social eating and derive a lot of pleasure from that. But if you eat just to survive and "keep going", like most people do, then the time you spend eating won't be that enjoyable and will have to be subtracted from your time winnings.

This will leave you with 48.5 years to live and enjoy life.

Grooming and Housework

You'll spend 1.8 years in the bathroom! This finding assumes the average person goes six times a day. Statistics also show that men spend four more minutes than women daily on the toilet—not clear why, but certainly not to contemplate the meaning of life!

Men spend around five months of their life shaving. So by growing a beard, men can reclaim that time.

Women, being the less hairy species, worry less about shaving. But they spend about one year of their life deciding what to wear—around fifteen minutes a day—and around five months applying makeup and dressing up for a night out. Of course, not all women fall into this category.

Women also spend about eighteen months of their life doing their hair. That's 14,000 hours of brushing, washing, straightening, curling, cutting, and blow drying! Women also shop a lot more than men, with a survey of approximately 2,000 women finding they spend 8.5 years of their lives on "retail therapy." But that's the extreme; it's closer to two years of shopping if you assume a conservative 6 hours of retail and grocery shopping each week from the age of 20.

Incidentally, and as a result of women's relentless effort to look attractive, the average man spends eleven months of his life staring at women! According to a U.K poll of 3,000 people, men spend on average forty-three minutes admiring around ten women every day.

Women also spend 3.6 years of their life on average doing housework. That includes cleaning the house, doing laundry, and cooking. The average for men is only half of that, making them the slightly less hygienic species.

If you have children under the age of six you'll spend an average of 2.1 hours each day providing childcare. If your children are between the ages of six and seventeen, you'll spend just 50 minutes a day on that. That is equivalent to 1.5 years until they are 18 years old.

If you add up the total time men and women spent on grooming, shopping, childcare, and housework, you will get a range of six to ten years. Let's take an average of 8 years for an average person during their life.

This leaves you with 40.5 years to live and enjoy your life.

Exercise

Exercise is essential for maintaining a healthy lifestyle and is considered a basic need. If you are an average American, you'll spend approximately one year of your life doing some form of exercise. This is based on a survey by the Center for Disease Control and Prevention (CDC) that analyzed data collected from more than 450,000 U.S. adults aged eighteen and older. They found American spend an average of 43 minutes a day in fitness and sports activities, while adults only perform 17 minutes a day. Similar results can be found in the U.K. and other European countries.

Therefore, the total time spent on basic needs—sleeping, grooming, housework, eating, and exercise—is 41.5 years. That's the time you'll invest to maintain and hopefully ensure your health, for without sleeping, eating, grooming, and exercise, you won't survive to enjoy the remaining years.

Taking care of yourself leaves you with 39.5 years for the other time categories: earning money and enjoying life.

Time Spent Generating Money

Education

You can't earn much money without having a minimum amount of education. In the U.S., you must attend school until you are eighteen years old. A standard school day is seven hours long. With five days a week and 13 school years to graduate—excluding weekends and summer breaks—you'll spend a total of 875 days studying, or 2.3 years of your life.

If you go to college, you'll probably spend three months of your life pursuing a college education. That's based on a study conducted by The

Heritage Foundation that found the average full-time college student spends only 2.76 hours a day on education-related activities. This amount includes both class time and studying, for an average of 19.3 hours each week. You'll be spending around 2,100 hours in learning—i.e., three months—over the course of a standard three-year college degree.

The total time spent on education is therefore 2.5 years on average. This leaves you with 37 years to earn money and enjoy life.

Working and Earning Money

Over a typical lifespan, you'll spend 10 years of your life working. This varies depending on the type of work that you do. The estimate is based on people who have a day job and work forty hours a week for most of their adult life until retirement age—a period of approximately 44 years—excluding weekends and two weeks of vacation each year.

For many office workers, it is estimated they'll spend around 5 years sitting at a desk. Work meetings, over the course of a typical career, consume around 2 years! A 2013 study[2] in *Management Today* found that more than a quarter of that time is wasted on pointless discussions. *That's six months of mind-numbing futility!*

Of course, the time we have to spend at work to support ourselves varies from one person to another. It depends on your actual income, expenditures, and any financial generosity or support from the rest of your family.

By subtracting the average time spent at work from your time winnings, you are left with 27 years to really enjoy life. It might be less than that depending on the kind of work you do. At the end of this chapter, there is a questionnaire that will help you calculate your own time usages.

Driving and Waiting

Driving or commuting to school, college, or the workplace is also part of the time needed to earn money. The average time you'll spend commuting or driving a car is around 4.3 years (excluding weekends), assuming you start driving from the age of 18 until you are 78 years old. This is based on a study done by the Harvard Health Watch[3] that found that the average American spends 101 minutes driving each day. A similar survey of British drivers found the average motorist spends 3.3 years of their life driving.

Incidentally, you'll cover a distance of 1.8 million kilometers over that period of time—enough to take you to the moon and back four times!

A recent survey by Realtor.com for the *New York Times* found that New Yorkers spend an hour and 15 minutes for a typical round-trip commute. Los Angeles and Washington D.C were not far off from that. In London, a survey by the Office for National Statistics showed the average daily commute is 2 hours for a round trip.

While driving, you'll typically sacrifice seven months waiting on traffic lights—that's two days of your life each year. It is worst in New York, were people waste a dreadful 89 hours each year in traffic congestion (that's 3.7 days each year)!

On top of that, and according to a survey of 20,000 motorists, you'll also spend an average of one year of your life in traffic jams, and eight months searching for a parking space or waiting in various lines.

Therefore, the time spent commuting and waiting adds up to around 6 years.

The total time you'll invest on education, commuting or driving, and earning money will be 18.5 years.

This leaves you with 21 years of free time that's available for leisure or anything you like.

The question is: how are *you* going to spend them?

Time Spent Enjoying Life—Generating Fun

Digital Media Consumption

The 2016 ATUS survey showed that men, on average, spent 5.5 hours each day in some form of leisure activity, whereas women spent 4.8 hours—44 minutes less than men). Of that time, watching TV accounted for half of the leisure time: 2.8 hours per day. This amount varies by age. People aged less than 44 years old watch two hours a day, while people over 65 watch TV for four hours a day. But on average, a typical American will watch around 80,486 hours—or more than 9 years' worth of TV in a lifetime! The only places where people watch more TV are Saudi Arabia, Croatia, Lithuania, Romania, and Serbia.

Out of those 9 years, 3 years are spent watching commercials! That's 3 years you are going to waste on someone trying to sell you toothpaste, cereals, and shampoo! But that is reducing now that many people stream TV through Netflix, Amazon Prime, Sling TV, and other similar services.

In fact, the trend in TV viewing time has been slowly declining compared to the expanding growth in digital media consumption. Most people who manage to watch less TV end up spending more time on the Internet. According to the latest statistics, the average American user spends up to 5 hours per day on mobile devices. The average around the world is four hours and twenty-five minutes a day. Half of that time is spent on social media, messaging, and entertainment applications.

YouTube comes in first, consuming more than 40 minutes of a person's day—or one year and ten months over a lifetime. Facebook users spend an average of 35 minutes a day. This totals one year and seven months of their life *posting social media updates about that life—instead of living it*!

Snapchat and Instagram come in next, with 25 minutes and 15 minutes spent per day, respectively. So on average, the average American will spend around 5.3 years of their life glued online to a digital screen… and that's likely to increase as smart devices only become more common in the future.

The total average amount of time you'll spend consuming media—watching TV, surfing the web, using an app on your phone, and so forth—is around 14 years of your life.

How much time would that leave you to truly enjoy life?

Just a mere seven year!

Time Remaining to Enjoy Life

Subtracting TV and media consumption time from the 21 years that are available as your leisure time will leave you with just seven years spread out over a seventy-eight-year lifespan to enjoy life. Sadly, this is all that's left for most people living a hectic lifestyle.

It's reality. Those seven years are all you have available in between the time you spend sleeping, eating, grooming, learning, earning money, driving, watching TV, and surfing the net. They are spread non-uniformly over your life. A couple of hours here and a few days there. They make up just 9 percent of an entire average lifespan. And take it from me: those are the most precious seven years of time you will have on this planet. This is where "all the magic" happens!

Life Essence - La Crème de la Crème

If you are able to squeeze out the very best of your life—la crème de la crème of the time you've won— this highly-concentrated extract will be those seven years—what I call your "*Life Essence*".

When all the "fluff" in a life is taken out, a typical lifetime is reduced to those seven years: your Life Essence. Think of it as *what constitutes your life story.*

If someone were to produce a movie about your life, it would be made up of scenes from those seven years.

When people on their deathbeds think back about their life and how meaningful it was, they usually talk about moments from those seven years.

It is *your* own personal time. It is your miracle time.

It is the time you use to create long-lasting memories; to engage in close and meaningful relationships; and to enjoy stimulating hobbies like writing, painting, sculpting, inventing, and horseback riding—or anything you're passionate about.

It is the time available for you to invest in yourself and learn new skills that will further your goals and dreams.

It is the time for creativity, inventions, literature, and art; the time in which you derive satisfaction from life.

It is the time you have to leave your mark on this world—and make it a better place.

Those are the years that make up your "paradise time."

If you believe in Heaven, time in paradise is an eternity that—depending on your belief—you'll spend playing the harp with some angels, or drinking wine with a few virgins, or in a state of nirvana, or perhaps something else.

But if you're not tied into any particular religious belief, then paradise time is that balance of time you'll spend enjoying your stay here on Earth after deducting all your *"time taxes."* More on that below.

When you think about time in this way, you realize how limited and scarce it is. Just 7 years and the clock is ticking!

If You Won the Powerball Tonight

If you won the $500 million Powerball jackpot tonight, how would you spend it?

A British study showed that winners spend a large chunk of their lottery winnings within just five years, and only a few manage to wisely spend their entire winnings over their whole lifetime. According to the National Endowment for Financial Education, more than half of the people who win a lottery end up broke in a few years. That's because winners suddenly realize they have an abundance of money that cost them practically nothing—and they start spending it recklessly. By the time they realize how much of their prize they've wasted, it is too late.

Isn't that somehow similar to our lottery-of-life prize? An average person "wins" 78 years of time to live their life. That lottery prize didn't really cost them anything. Other than being extremely lucky—a true miracle—they did not have to *do* anything to be born. But then think of it this way: they'll spend most of their "time winnings" on satisfying basic needs, earning money, and consuming media. It ends up being akin to the hefty taxes a Powerball lottery winner has to pay before they can enjoy their prize!

Depending on the state where the lottery is won, winners end up paying up to 40 percent in taxes on their winnings to the government. When it comes to the lottery of life, a person will pay around 91 percent of their time winnings in the form of **time taxes** before they can enjoy the true prize: their take-home Life Essence years!

Your precious "free time" is actually not free after all. It comes at the heavy price of 71 years in **time taxes** you have to "pay" to enjoy those 7 **life essence** years.

Sadly, a lot of people don't even know they are winners. They go through life without appreciating how precious and limited the time (prize) they won is—until it is too late. It takes them a whole lifetime to realize they've did not use it wisely.

By then, it's too late, and so they rush to "make up" the difference in the remaining years that are left. A multi-billion-dollar self-help industry has flourished on the hope that, even though we cannot create more time, we can at least make the most of what we have. The books that have been written on time management, productivity, procrastination, and habits all essentially advise us on how to do more in less time. While that sounds great for achievements and success, it's not the solution. Read on.

How to Assess Your Life Essence Years

The first step is to gain awareness of how much time you as an individual spend on the categories of basic needs, earning money, and enjoying life. To do that, you'll need an objective system of measurement that tracks your time so that you get a healthy dose of reality. Once you garner an understanding of how valuable your time really is, you can start making appropriate changes to your lifestyle so that you spend time *more efficiently.*

Let's start with some time-measurement systems and complete the following "Time Miracle Task."

Time Miracle Task

Complete the following:

A. Estimate your lifespan, based on your health criteria.

B. Calculate how you spend time on your various needs (fill below questionnaire or click on this Life Essence Evaluation form.

C. Estimate your Life Essence years.

A. Estimate Your Lifespan

To estimate how many years you *personally* won in terms of your lifespan (and not the just "average person's" 78 years), check the online diagnostic tool below. Based on your health criteria, it will estimate your expected lifespan and how long you still have to live.

https://www.livingto100.com/calculator/start/1

Those are the remaining years that's left of your life lottery winnings.

B. Calculate How You Spend your Time

To estimate how *you* spend *your* time, use the categories for basic needs, earning money, and life enjoyment so you can assess the value of these time taxes and the balance of life essence.

1. **Basic Needs**
   - Sleeping: How many hours do you sleep on a typical day? _____hours
   - Eating: Add up the time you spend on average for your breakfast, lunch, and dinner: _____ hours
   - Time spent grooming each day (bathroom, shower): _____ hours
   - Hours spent on housework per day:_____ hours
   - Hours spent shopping per day (estimate hours spent shopping per week and divide by 7):_____ hours
   - Hours spent on exercise per day (estimate hours spent per week and divide by 7): _____ hours

   Now add up all the hours spend on basic needs per day, then divide by 24 to obtain the proportion of a typical day spent on basic needs. Multiply that fraction by the estimated remaining number of years available for you to live and you will get the number of years you will spend on basic needs.

2. **Earning Money**
   a. <u>Education:</u>
   - Are you still in college? Yes_____ No_____
   - If yes, how many years do you have to graduate? _____years
   - How many hours do you spend in college in a year (hours spent per term multiplied by the number of terms per year)?_____ hours

- Multiply that the time spent per year by the number of years to graduate, then divide that by 8,760 (number of hours in a year), and you will obtain the number of years you actually spent in education.

b. Work:
- How many hours do you work each day? _____ hours
- How many days do you work in a typical month? _____ days
- Multiply the hours per day by how many days per month and the multiply the total by 12 to get the total hours you spend at work in a typical year.
- How many years do you think you have until you retire? _____ years
- Multiply those years by the total number of hours you work each year and you will get the total hours you will spend at work until you retire. Divide that by 8,760 and you will obtain the number of your remaining years you will spend at work.

c. Driving & Commuting:
- Do you drive or commute to work?
- If yes, how many hours do you typically spend driving/ commuting in a day? _____ hours
- Multiply that by the number of years until you retire and divide by 24 to obtain the number of years you will spend driving or commuting.

3. **Media Consumption**
   - How many hours do you spend watching TV each day (on average)? _____ hours
   - How many hours do you spend online (on social media or surfing the web) each day? _____ hours

Now add then up and divide by 24 to obtain the proportion of a typical day spent on media consumption. Multiply that fraction by the estimated remaining number of years available for you to live and you will get the number of years you will spend on media consumption

Calculate Your Time Taxes_____

Add up the number of years you spend on basic needs, education, work, and driving or commuting, and media consumption to estimate your total "time tax" years.

C. **Estimate Your Life Essence Years**
   Now to calculate the number of years available for enjoying life, subtract your "time taxes," (i.e., the total number of years spent on basic needs, earning money, driving or commuting, media consumption, etc.) from the estimated number of years you have to live and you will obtain the amount of time you really have to enjoy life.

These are your life essence years_____

Life Essence Evaluation Online Form

If you are reading this as an e-book, you can click on the <u>Life Essence Evaluation online form</u> to calculate your **life essence years**

Or use the following link:

<u>https://goo.gl/forms/dW9gBLBbDi1XQtms1</u>

Here is another Time Miracle task for your consideration.

Time Miracle Task

What Constitutes Your Life Story?

_____

_____

_____

List the top 10 Most Important Scenes from the Movie of Your Life: Your Life Essence Moments.

1. _____

2. _____

3. _____

4. _____

5. _____

6. _____

7. _____

8. _____

9. _____

10. _____

3

The Most Valuable Resource

Time's True Value

∽

"To lament that we shall not be alive a hundred years from now,
is the same folly as to be sorry we were not alive a hundred
years ago."

– Montaigne

The Tiny Spotlight

Scientists almost unanimously agree that time began when the Universe
blew up in a Big Bang about 15 billion years ago. The Earth has been
around for about 4.5 billion years, and life on Earth started around 3.8
billion years ago, mostly with microbes and bacteria. The first species of
fish appeared around 530 million years ago, followed by land plants (475
million years ago), and mammals (around 200 million years ago).

Our species, Homo sapiens, has been around for about 200,000 years
only—constituting a mere 0.004 percent of Earth's history. During this
time, around 120 billion people have already lived and died, and around

7 billion people are still alive today. So that means… *around 95 percent of all people who have ever lived are no longer here!* They will never be able to see another sunset again or kiss their children goodnight. But you… *you* are one of the lucky ones: one of the 5 percent life-lottery winners who are alive today.

Based on the average rate of extinction, scientists estimate that humans will almost certainly be extinct in around 8 million years (that is, if we manage to refrain from obliterating ourselves with our nuclear toys and let nature takes it course). In theory, humans should continue to exist for another 8 million years.

Now let us imagine there is one immensely long tunnel that represents the whole timeline of human existence. The "present" has been traveling from the past towards the future like a tiny spotlight crawling its way along that vast tunnel of darkness. Everything that lies behind that spotlight is an eternity of total darkness: the darkness of the dead past. Everything ahead of that spotlight is immersed in the darkness of the unknown future.

The miracle moment you won the lottery of life, you happened to be born in the spotlight representing your century—your present generation. It is within that short period of time that you will open your eyes and explore the world around you. The time you have before the light goes off is on average 78 years, most of which you will spend sleeping, eating, working, and watching TV. You know you'll only live once, and therefore have only one shot at this.

So… how are you going to use that chance? How are you going to spend that priceless prize? And how valuable is that time?

Should You Save Time or Money?

When people evaluate their time, most would simply calculate the total earnings they make in one year and divide that by the number of hours they worked during that time. What they get then is their average hourly wage per year.

Let us say you spend 2,500 hours annually earning money. If you make $12,060 per year, your time is worth $4.82 per hour and you would be on the 2017 poverty line for an individual living in the United States. If, on the other hand, you make $100,000 annually, your time is worth $40 per hour.

Equating time with money is useful in a few practical situations. Let us say you are shopping online for a purse, and you find what you are looking at the affordable price of $20. The bag is produced in the United Kingdom, and it would cost $50 to ship it to the United States. Chances are you would probably be turned off by the idea of paying $50 to ship a $20 item.

But let us say that the bag is also available in a store in a close-by city (only an hour's drive away) and the questions in your mind are these: Is an hour of your time worth $50? Should you save time, and pay $50 to get the bag shipped to you? Or, should you save cash, and spend one hour of your time driving to pick up the bag in person?

Questions such as this, wherein we weigh the value of what to do, pop up all the time in our minds: should we purchase a nonstop flight and save two hours, or get the flight with the stopover and save $100? Should we pay our neighbor's teenager $20 to mow our lawn so we can have an extra hour free on the weekend? The answer to such questions depends on our hourly wages. We make such choices every day, basing the decisions mostly on gut feelings.

But we would make different choices if we actually *know* what our time is worth. For example, if we know our time is worth $30 per hour, we generally would choose not to wait an hour in line just to get a $10 discount. If we *know* our time is worth $70 per hour, we usually would choose to pay $50 for shipping instead of driving an hour (valued at $70) to shop for the bag in a store.

Knowing your hourly wage is also useful for *reallocating time,* so as to make better use of it. How many times have you spent a long time doing something that you could have paid an expert to do more efficiently for you? For example, you don't know how to fix your car, but you spend a few hours attempting to figure it out, rather than paying a mechanic to fix it for you. Because you value *money* more than *time,* you would rather waste your time versus spend money on the mechanic.

This kind of thing happens all the time. But you might change your mind about who should perform the task if you know how valuable your time is and recognize there are more important things you could enjoy with that "wasted time."

The Picasso Perspective

Studies confirm that people are happier when they spend their money on saving time, as compared to buying more material stuff. But to make wise decisions like that, we need to understand that the money we spend on the mechanic is not just for the couple of hours he worked on our car, but for all the years it took him to become an expert mechanic.

There is a story of a woman who approached Picasso one day while he was sitting in a park and asked him to make a portrait of her. Picasso agreed and quickly drew her portrait. When she saw it, she was very pleased and asked him how much she owed him. Picasso replied,

"$5,000." The woman was taken back and said, "$5,000 is a lot, and it only took you a few minutes to draw this!" "No, ma'am," Picasso replied, "It took me my entire life."

What this teaches us is that reallocating our time by outsourcing expert advice makes better use of it. Various studies have shown that having more free time will make you happier than having more money. Successful people know that, and often pay for expert advice to help them save time and achieve their goals faster. For them, time is valued more highly than money. They understand that the natural urge to "save money" will actually end up costing them more.

More importantly, they appreciate that time has an "opportunity cost," and they take that into consideration when making critical decisions.

A Time Miracle Tip

Work out your hourly wage here _____ **$ per hour**

List the top 5 things you could outsource to save on your precious time:

1. _____

2. _____

3. _____

4. _____

5. _____

Our Most Valuable Resource

What we saw so far is only the monetary value of time, i.e., how much money we can generate by spending it. That's not the true value of time.

Time's value comes from one of its unique qualities: mainly that it cannot be replenished. Once time is consumed, it cannot be regained. This makes it the most valuable resource—*way more precious than money.*

Just think about the fact that you can always earn more money by working longer hours, but you cannot do anything to earn more time. Also, when you spend your time on one thing, you give up the opportunity to spend it on other things. Any benefit that might have been derived had you chosen to do any of those other things is lost forever.

Moreover, time cannot be saved for later use. Unlike a monetary lottery prize that you can save in a bank, you have no choice but to spend every moment of your time winnings—*and every moment spent is a moment that's gone forever.*

But if time is more precious than money, why do we spend it as if it costs us nothing? Most of us wouldn't mind "wasting" a couple of hours doing nothing but would be very upset if we lost a couple of hundred dollars from our wallet. *If we are so careful in how and where we spend our money, why do we fail to do the same with time?* The answer lies in how abundant we perceive time to be, and how fast we perceive it to be passing. This perception varies as we go through life and is best explained by two principles:

- The Marginal Utility Theory of Economics
- The Dynamic of Dread and Desire (DDD)

Diamonds are a Girl's Best Friend (or are They?)

The father of economics, Adam Smith, was baffled by a paradox that goes like this: *we cannot survive without water, but we can get by without diamonds, yet we value diamonds much more highly than we do water; how can that be?*

The answer that economists give is that the value of a resource does not depend on the cost to produce it, but more on its ability to satisfy a human need. Value is a subjective thing, after all. This is known as the "Marginal Utility Theory."

To best understand it, let's say that a farmer can harvest five sacks of corn each year. The farmer needs the first sack to survive until the next harvest, so he is very careful with it. The second sack is not as crucial to the farmer's survival, but he appreciates it, as its existence ensures he will eat well. The third sack he uses to raise some chicken, as the resulting food source will provide variety to his diet. The fourth sack is a surplus, and so the farmer may use it to make some whiskey. The fifth sack is even more of a surplus, and he may use it to feed his pet birds.

In this example, the fifth sack of corn has the lowest value to the farmer. It would not matter much to him if he loses it (of course, his pet birds might have a different opinion). If he loses another sack, he would not be able to make whiskey, which would disappoint on a cold winter's evening, but not be as bad as losing a third sack. Without a third sack, the farmer would not be able to enjoy omelets for breakfast and chicken fingers for lunch. Now he would have to live basically on cornbread and corn soup until the next harvest. And if he were to lose that fifth and final sack, it would compromise his very ability to survive.

As the farmer loses one sack after another, the value of the remaining sacks of corn rises. By the time he has only one sack, its value would be extremely high, since losing it might lead to the farmer's starvation.

If we apply the Marginal Utility Theory to time, we would have to value time more like water than diamonds. It would be valued cheaply early in life when it seems plentiful, but it rises in value as we grow older and it gets scarce.

When we were young, we thought time was infinite—and so we did not really care how we spent it. But as we grow older and spend more from our "time winnings," time becomes less available—and so we will give it more value. Every second becomes more valuable than the one that preceded it.

Once you realize this basic truth of life, you will never allow time to "slip away" unused.

Dread vs. Desire

Another aspect of the value of time is *the speed at which it passes*. We know rationally that clocks tick at a constant rate—but emotions play a role in the speed at which we experience time. We do not experience time passing at a consistent rate: our anticipation and desires slow down time, whereas our negative anticipation, or dread, speeds it up. I call this (get ready), "The Dynamic of Dread and Desire."

Doesn't time just seem to *dragggggggg* when we are expecting something nice to happen? The time leading up to the start of a weekend or vacation, or even a date, seems to take forever! The weekend just never seems to get here! Clearly, anticipating a pleasant event causes time to slow down.

But when we are dreading an upcoming event, the opposite occurs: that dentist appointment or audit arrives way faster than you hoped, right?

Studies confirm that future events expected to end with a loss appear to arrive faster than future events expected to end with a gain.[4] Just imagine you are watching your favorite soccer team playing the last five minutes of the World Cup final. They are in the lead, 1–0, and the opposing team is pressing hard. You obviously want those last five minutes to pass by quickly before the other team gets a chance to tie up the game. But time crawls at an agonizing pace as you eagerly anticipate that final whistle.

Now, let's imagine it's the other way round: your team is down 0–1 in those last five minutes, and you are wishing (praying!) the game time stretches on and on, for as long as possible. You want the time to "slow down" so as to postpone the final whistle and give your team a chance to tie or win the game. Instead, it feels like your team is racing against the clock; as if the time to the game's end simply flew by.

Our desire slows down time; our dread speeds it up. And this applies to how we see ourselves in relation to time: the greater the desire for a pleasant future event, the further away in time it seems. The more we dread something, the nearer in times it seems and the faster it arrives. I am sure you can think of many instances in your life where you experienced that.

When Your Whole Life was Ahead of You

Now let's apply this principle to your whole lifespan.

When you were young, your whole life was still ahead of you. You lived mostly in the future. As a child, you didn't care about wasting time, because you thought time was infinite. You were eager to grow up and were constantly anticipating something good to happen. You just "couldn't wait" to become a teenager, or go to high school or college—and yet, didn't it just seem to take *forever* to happen?

Young students are so eager to graduate, get their first car or job, and become independent. This desire for a pleasant future causes time to drag. This is one of the reasons why time appears to run so slowly in childhood, when compared to middle and old age. The feeling that time is running slowly creates the perception that it is abundant and, therefore, less valuable. This mindset often leads to many wasted youth years.

In contrast, when you are older you slowly start to live in the past, recalling accomplishments and misfortunes from your younger years. When you reach your fifties and sixties, the greater portion of your life now lies behind you. You no longer anticipate life's most important milestones, such as school graduation, your first job, marriage, or children, as most of these have been transformed into memories. As you draw closer to the end of your life, time appears to move faster as you struggle to slow it down. As time "speeds up" for you in this way, you'll come to feel it is scarce—and, therefore, more valuable.

Faster and Faster!

The only time when you mostly live in the present is middle age—so that's when you appreciate the true value of time. As former President Theodore Roosevelt put it, "The only time you really live fully is from thirty to sixty. The young are slaves to dreams; the old servants of regrets. Only the middle-aged have all their five senses in the keeping of their wits."

In brief, by applying the Dynamic of Dread and Desire to a whole lifetime, we understand why time speeds up and increases in value as we grow older. *How we feel about the future affects our perception of time.* When the future outlook is positive, time slows down; when the outlook is negative, time speeds up. As we grow up, the available time for us diminishes, and thus it becomes more valuable. However, this diminishing rate is not constant: time speeds up, and the rate at which we lose time accelerates, making it even more valuable.

An hour at birth has practically no value to you as compared against the infinitely more valuable last hour of your life before you depart.

Maximize Your Return

The goal of any successful entrepreneur is to invest money so as to maximize profit, or what is known as the "Return on Investment." Similarly, to live a fulfilling life, your goal is to *maximize the return on your time invested.* After all, life is short, and if you have a full-time job and kids, it will feel hard, if not impossible, to move toward your dreams and experience the "time of your life." Unless you organize your time and maximize your

Life Essence efficiently, you'll get lost in your increasingly demanding life. Before you know it, you'll be wondering how "time just flew by."

In my first book The Power of Time Perception, I explored in detail how our subjective experience of the speed of time depends on our age, anxiety level, whether you are a morning or night person, an introvert or extrovert, how easily you get bored, and the culture you grew up in. To find your current experienced speed of time, check out the following link or click on the online Speed of Time Test.

https://goo.gl/forms/3bqt8nAVQIJQ7BXM2

By answering a few questions, you will receive a detailed report about how fast time runs in your mind!

Here's a little reflection that can help you get started on generating a strong "return."

For that, go ahead and complete the following "Time Miracle Task."

Time Miracle Task

How much of your time are you in complete control of? (Provide a rough daily percentage.) _____

Are you spending most of your time furthering your own dreams, or someone else's? If so, whose? _____

How much of your time are you wasting on things you don't intrinsically enjoy (on a daily, monthly, and yearly basis)?

_____

What are the Top 5 activities *you should remove* from your life? Which ones are you *actually able to*?

1. _____
2. _____
3. _____
4. _____
5. _____

What dreams did you have for your life when you were young?

_____

_____

_____

If life continues as it is now, what regrets would you have in the end?

1. _____

2. _____

3. _____

4. _____

5. _____

How can you claim back some "time tax rebates" so you are able to use more of your prize winnings? How can you individually reduce your Time Taxes and increase your Life Essence? It's clear you still have to sleep, eat, earn money, but is there a way to optimize those time expenditures?

The next book section will deal with ways to maximize your "Life Essence" by:

- Reclaiming sleep time
- Reclaiming eating time
- Reclaiming exercise time
- Reclaiming work time
- Reclaiming media consumption time

PART TWO

SQUEEZE MORE
OUT OF LIFE!

4

Quality Sleep Hacks

Reclaim 3 Years!

∽

"We are such stuff as dreams are made on; and our little life is
rounded with a sleep."
– William Shakespeare

The Sleep Myth

Sleep is critical to your overall physical and mental health: a good
night's sleep can increase your ability to solve complex problems by
50 percent. It will improve your memory, lower your stress, boost your
ability to focus, enhance your creativity, and lengthen your life. Sleep
enhances athletic performance and can improve your ability to learn new
motor skills by 20 percent.

In contrast, inadequate amounts of sleep can lead to obesity. It will
make you feel weak, clumsy, and, in some cases, plain old stupid. Getting
enough sleep is an awesome thing.

Now, we've all heard that eight hours of sleep is the "recommended"
magic number for adults. The problem is that this amount of sleep
consumes a third of every one of our days, and therefore, a third of our

life. If we live to the age of 78, we'll be sound asleep for 26 years! Is there a way to reclaim some of that time back into our life?

Fortunately, recent research suggests the need to get eight hours of sleep every night is just a myth. A recent study[5] concluded that *sleeping as little as six and a half hours per night is actually better than sleeping for eight!*

Researchers from the University of California–San Diego spent six years tracking the amount of sleep of 1.1 million people aged 30-102 years old[6]. They found no health-related benefits for sleeping more than 6.5 hours per night. In fact, those who slept between 6.5 and 7.4 hours lived longer than those who slept longer than 7.4 hours or less than 6.5 hours.

Another two-year study[7] from the respected National Sleep Foundation that reviewed more than 300 scientific publications from top sleep gurus also concluded that the appropriate amount of sleep can be as low as seven hours. The National Heart, Lung, and Blood Institute published similar findings.

In another study[8] from the University of California–Los Angeles, scientists studied the sleep habits of three hunter–gatherer tribes from Namibia, Tanzania, and Bolivia. Those tribes were chosen because their traditional lifestyles are thought to be similar to that of our ancestors. The results showed that the villagers slept for an average of just 6.5 hours per night—and were less obese and healthier than people in modern societies. Of course, factors other than sleep hours affect these results, but the common conclusion from all these studies is that what mattered most is not the number of hours you sleep, but the *quality of sleep you are getting*. A 10-hour sleep might be worth just two hours of high-quality sleep if you wake up 10 times during the night. Sleep quality is the key that will help you reclaim more of that time back into your life essence.

For instance, if you are 30 years old now and start sleeping 6.5 hours of high-quality sleep instead of eight hours, you will be reclaiming 1.5 hours each day back into your "Life Essence."

Over the next 50 years or so, this will add up to around 3 extra years of valuable time which otherwise would have been spent in dreamland! But again, the key to making this work is to *improve sleep quality over quantity.*

Quality Sleep Hacks

The stress of modern living has made it harder to get the quality sleep that we need to function properly. We get tired easily, experience mood swings that border on depression, and, as a result, our bodies struggle to cope. Reports suggest that insomnia affects up to 80 percent of the population. Many people resort to sleeping pills. Sleep-aid prescriptions have tripled since the late '90s. But studies found that sleeping pills actually increase the probability of dying earlier. This means you are better off suffering through sleepless nights than popping sleeping pills and suddenly losing all your life lottery time winnings. Fortunately, there are safer ways to enhance sleep time and reclaim those 3 years. I call it, "Quality Sleep Hacking."

Here are a few tips from the National Sleep Foundation:

- **Block all light sources and sleep in a pitch-black room.** Make the room as dark as possible. If you live in a city, use blackout curtains to prevent light pollution.
- **Set your room temperature to 65 degrees Fahrenheit** (18.5 degrees Celsius) **or lower.** Research confirms that sleeping in a cold room is better for your health. Your room should be like

a cold, dark, and quiet cave—the same kind of environment in which your ancestors slept a hundred thousand years ago.

- **Invest in a comfortable mattress and pillow.**
- **Don't eat late.** If you try to sleep while your body is still digesting food, you won't get quality sleep, and you will wake up feeling worse.
- **Stop drinking caffeine at least eight hours prior to bedtime**, by around 3:00 p.m. each day.
- **Stick to a sleep schedule, even on weekends.** The ideal time is to go to bed before 11:00 p.m.
- **As you get ready for bed, practice a relaxing bedtime ritual.** Start winding down at least two hours before bed. Turn off electronics, the TV, computer screens, and mobile phones, and preferably do some reading to relax. It also would be best if you could remove all tablets, smartphones, and other computer-related devices from your bedroom. If that is not possible, at least dim them, because the light that emanates is distracting and interferes with quality sleep. You also can install a program called *f.lux* on your PC or Mac that will automatically adjust screen brightness with the time of the day (many cell phones offer an option like this in Settings now, and some phones do it automatically). Don't look at electronic screens at least thirty minutes before bedtime.

Transforming Night Owls into Early Birds

In her book *What the Most Successful People Do Before Breakfast*, Laura Vanderkam interviewed twenty top executives and found that 90 percent said they wake up before six a.m., including:

- Disney CEO Bob Iger arises at 4:30 a.m. to read.

- Twitter CEO Jack Dorsey starts jogging at 5:30 in the morning.
- PepsiCo CEO Indra Nooyi wakes at four a.m. and is in the office by 7 a.m.
- Richard Branson, founder of the Virgin Group, gets up at 5:45 a.m.
- Apple CEO Tim Cook starts sending work-related emails at 4:30 a.m.
- Howard Schultz, former Starbucks CEO, wakes up before 5:00 a.m.

According to Mason Currey's book *Daily Rituals*, Ludwig Beethoven, John Milton, Charles Dickens, Franz Kafka, Kurt Vonnegut, Maya Angelou, Honoré de Balzac, Le Corbusier, Voltaire, and Victor Hugo were all early risers who began their creative projects early in the morning. *Early risers consistently begin their day more focused and ready for action.*

Now, if you are a night owl, training yourself to wake up early so you become an early bird should be done *gradually*. Here's how:

- **Start with minor tweaks, slowly shifting your wake-up time so that your body adapts to the new routine.** Cut back a few minutes each morning—setting your alarm clock to, say, 7:45 a.m. instead of 8:00. After a few days or a week of that, aim for 7:30 a.m. That way, you won't feel tired during the day.
- **Put the alarm across the room so that you have to get out of bed to turn it off.** (But if you have a partner, that might not be a good idea! In that case, a soft alarm next to your bed would be better.)
- **Don't hit the snooze, ever.** Those extra few minutes of sleep are a waste of time, as they cloud your thinking and after your mind

will start ignoring the clamor of the alarm. Your mindset should be that of being excited about your day and ready to jump out of bed.

- **Once you reach your new desired waking-up time, make it a habit to wake up at the same time every day.** Your body becomes conditioned and starts regulating your sleep pattern so that you actually begin the waking-up process long before the alarm goes off. In time, this becomes natural, and you won't need an alarm clock to wake up.

Harness Your Subconscious Power

What you do before you go to bed the night before has a significant impact on your next day. Hal Elrod writes in his popular book, *Miracle Morning:*

How you wake up each day and your morning routine (or lack thereof) dramatically affect your levels of success in every single area of your life. Focused, productive, successful mornings generate focused, productive, successful days—which inevitably create a successful life—in the same way that unfocused, unproductive, and mediocre mornings generate unfocused, unproductive, and mediocre days, and ultimately a mediocre quality of life. By simply changing the way you wake up in the morning, you can transform any area of your life, faster than you ever thought possible.

Almost all successful people write down in the evening up to three of the most important things they want to accomplish the next day. **So,**

ten minutes before you sleep, meditate on any questions or challenges you want to accomplish and *write them down*. Ask yourself questions related to those things too: your subconscious mind never rests and following this practice will allow it to start working on those tasks while you're asleep. Often, you'll wake up to find all the answers already in your head!

Thomas Edison, arguably America's greatest inventor, said, "Never go to sleep without a request to your subconscious." It will help you focus your next day and give you something to look forward to when you wake up.

Adopt "the Perfect" Morning Routine

There are hundreds of great books out there about the benefits of morning routines and habits. All agree that mastering your daily morning ritual will not only set the tone for the rest of your day but also is the foundation for a successful life.

Here's how you can perfect your morning routine:

- **After you wake up in the morning, resist the temptation to check your smartphone notifications** (like most people do). It just distracts your subconscious mind.
- **Thought-dump immediately.** Within ten minutes of getting up, find a quiet place and reflect on what your subconscious has been working on overnight. Read through the questions you wrote the night before, then write down whatever answers come to mind in a process called "thought-dumping."

Research confirms that *the brain is most active and creative immediately after you wake up.* In those first few minutes, you'll be able to tap into an unprecedented level of creativity and problem-solving skills. Channeling your thinking in that way will create the conditions for success and achieving your goals.

- **Engage in some of the very best morning habits**: working out, reading, learning something new, spending time with your loved ones, or working on your "passion projects." The things you can do with the one or two free hours you've gleaned from becoming an efficient "early bird" can vary from short-time goals—a quick workout—to long-term goals—improving your health through eating a nutritious breakfast and meditating to de-stress. As a reminder, refrain from checking emails, news, or social media, as these will only distract you from your primary goals.

  Thirty minutes in the morning is an ideal time to exercise: running, swimming, walking, yoga, Pilates. By starting your day with exercise, you'll prevent yourself from putting it off later on.

  Or, start a "passion hobby" or side project that eventually becomes your life's achievement. Many successful people put in an hour on personal projects before they formally start their day. The project could be something you've always wanted to do, but never had the time to do it. Or, it could be even a new skill you want to learn that will help you later on.

- **Get "the big work" done early.** If you want to get straight onto your work, focus on the high-priority tasks first. Have you ever heard Mark Twain's famous quote, "Eat a live frog first thing in the morning and nothing worse will happen to you the rest of the day"? This means that if you start on your difficult tasks first, the rest of your day will look pretty good by comparison.

  Many studies have shown that our willpower is highest in the morning and dwindles as the day goes by. Mornings also tend to offer the least distractions, so it's the best time to focus on important projects without being interrupted by kids, employees, bosses, etc.

- **Do a Steve Jobs.** In a commencement address at Stanford University, the Apple co-founder said this about motivating himself:

  For the past 33 years, I have looked in the mirror every morning and asked myself: 'If today were the last day of my life, would I want to do what I am about to do today?' And whenever the answer has been no for too many days in a row, I know I need to change something.

  If you ask yourself that same question each and every morning, the resulting answer will give you an indication of what you need to work on, and what new things you may want to introduce into your morning routine that will eventually help you make your desired change in your life.

  Jobs' advice is a great motivational tactic for all.

Nap it Up!

Okay, okay, we've talked about morning productivity and routines; well, what about the rest of your day?

It turns out, if you really feel sleepy during the day, giving back a quick nap is not such a bad thing. Research has shown that short naps of 10 to 15 minutes can dramatically increase learning, memory, creativity, and productivity.

Albert Einstein, Thomas Edison, Winston Churchill, John F. Kennedy, Leonardo da Vinci, Napoleon Bonaparte, Ronald Reagan, Lyndon B. Johnson, John D. Rockefeller, and Margaret Thatcher all took regular afternoon naps.

This might seem to contradict the advice of sleeping less and trying to reclaim every moment we can, but a 15-minutes nap in the afternoon will refresh your brain so that the rest of day i more productive and enjoyable.

Three Years, Reclaimed

Sleep takes the biggest portion of time spent out of all the basic needs. Practicing sleep hacking is easy and free, yet the overwhelming majority of people fail to do this. Yet the habit of waking up early will have the biggest impact on your life, because it allows you to focus several hours on yourself and your primary goals.

Good quality sleep means a healthier mind and body, and more importantly, you reclaim three years back out of the 26 years you would've spent sleeping. That's plenty of time to move towards your dreams!

Just imagine what you can do in those extra free hours you gain every morning. Once you start experiencing those benefits, you'll never sleep late again.

Time Miracle Task

Before you go to sleep, write down 3 important questions or challenges you want to accomplish the next day.

1. _____

2. _____

3. _____

As you go through your day, do you notice any difference in getting things done?

_____

_____

_____

5

Mindful Eating Hacks

Reclaim 3.5 Years

❧

"Time is the school in which we learn,
Time is the fire in which we burn."
– Delmore Schwartz

How Well are You Aging?

We all have friends from our age group that look years younger (or older) than we do. Such perceptions aren't just about physical looks, but more about the different pace at which each of us ages.

Aging doesn't happen overnight, but gradually over a period of decades. Much like water shaping riverbanks over time, aging is not obvious on a day-to-day basis—but its effects can be dramatic after a period of several years.

The speed at which you age depends on several factors including your blood pressure, lung function, cholesterol levels, body mass index, diet, and genes. Only 20 percent of the factors influencing aging are genetic, and as much as 80 percent are well within your control. These involve habits like a healthy diet, reducing stress, getting regular exercise and quality sleep, not smoking, and maintaining a healthy weight. Let's start with diet.

A Sandwich in One Hand & the Wheels in the Other

We already know that the average American spends 67 minutes a day on "primary" eating and drinking (meaning, our attention is directed on our meal), with the total time spent eating over the course of a lifetime being around 3.5 years. This does not take into account about 34 minutes per day spent on food preparation and cleanup.

In addition to that, the average American spends 24 minutes daily on "secondary" eating time, such as snacking while watching TV or doing something on the computer, having lunch at our desk; or driving while eating our meal one-handed. With secondary eating, we pay almost no attention to what or how much we are taking in.

Adding these eating times up, the average American spends around 80 minutes eating each day and will take in approximately one ton of food each year, according to the U.S. Department of Agriculture. Over a lifetime, about 80 tons of food are consumed.

Most of what we choose to eat is cheese, sweets, dense potatoes, fats— i.e. mostly unhealthy stuff—with more than three-fourths of the U.S population's diet being low in vegetables and fruits. At least one-quarter of Americans eat some type of fast food every day, and most Americans exceed the recommended amounts of sugars, saturated fats, and sodium.

Is it any surprise that most Americans are overweight? 37 percent of the nation's adult population is considered obese (with a BMI more than 30). This used to be 19 percent back in 1997. 69 percent is considered overweight (with a BMI more than 25).

It is not that better in the U.K with 28 percent of adults considered obese and 62 percent considered overweight, according to data published by the World Health Organization (WHO) in 2014.

MIND Your Longevity

What kind of diet are *you* living on? One of mostly fast food?

What are the consequences of that to your health?

Do you take your body for granted?

If you're still in your twenties or thirties, the effects of an unhealthy diet may not be immediate but disregarding your health will eventually catch up with you. Eating unhealthy food is like putting low-grade gas in a Ferrari or driving your car when the engine oil light is flashing.

Your body is the vehicle that carries you around, and through it you express your life. *When something goes wrong with your body, your whole life will be affected—including how much time you have left.* But when you take better care of your health, you will add many years to your precious time. One key to better health is eating healthy on a consistent basis.

It is generally accepted that diet has a 30 percent effect on how long we live. Studies show that some healthy diets can add as much as a decade to your life! Healthy eating also affects your brain's health, and that is obviously essential for you to enjoy life.

Some of the longest observed lifespans are for people living along the Mediterranean coast. The climate is perfect for abundant fruits, vegetables, olives, beans, and fish. These are all rich in anti-oxidants that combat aging and fight against inflammation. A U.S. study[9] that has been tracking the health and eating habits of more than 120,000 registered nurses since 1976 found that those who ate a Mediterranean diet were healthier than those who ate diets heavier in red meats and dairy products.

Another popular diet that received a lot of attention recently is the MIND diet. It was developed at Rush University Medical Center through a study funded by the National Institute on Aging. The goal was to lower the risk of Alzheimer's disease—a common kind of dementia that causes loss of memory and other cognitive abilities, thereby interfering with daily living— by promoting a diet consisting of brain-healthy foods. MIND is a hybrid combination of the Mediterranean and DASH (Dietary Approaches to Stop Hypertension) diets, and as such, emphasizes these ten brain-healthy foods, from both the Mediterranean and DASH diets:

- leafy greens
- vegetables
- nuts
- berries
- beans
- whole grains
- fish,
- poultry
- olive oil
- wine, in moderation

The MIND diet limits the intake of red meat, butter and margarine, cheese, pastries and sweets, and fried or fast food.

Studies showed the MIND diet cuts people's risk of Alzheimer's by an average of 53 percent. The longer a person stuck to the diet, the better protected he was from developing Alzheimer's. Keeping a healthy memory is also great for those precious memorable moments we collect over the years and make up our life story.

Other studies also showed that the MIND diet lowered the risk of heart disease *and significantly contributed to longevity.*

For more details about the MIND diet, check the link below or click here to download a FREE copy of my eBook, *The Ultimate Guide to a Healthy Brain Diet*. This will give you the main brain "superfoods" that are essential for your brain's health.

http://www.subscribepage.com/brain-diet

Remember, a healthy diet might not be the Fountain of Youth—but it may be the river that leads to it.

Speed Eating

It's not just our diet that is to blame for the obesity epidemic in America. One of the main reasons why obesity in the U.S. is on the rise has to do with how fast we eat.

Most Americans eat too fast, and as a result, they take in too many calories before they realize they've eaten enough. Man's digestive system is such that it takes about twenty minutes for the stomach to send back signals telling the brain it has received enough food and doesn't need anymore. If you are speed-eating, you will keep eating beyond the point when you should feel "full." By the time the signal finally reaches your brain, it's already too late; you would have swallowed the last bite of that second helping, and started on a slice of Death by Chocolate!

When you eat fast, you also tend to underestimate how much you ate, especially if it is "secondary" distracted eating. In addition to making you fat, eating fast causes indigestion because you are not chewing your food well enough. Lazy chewing sends all that food hurtling down before it is ready for your stomach to receive it. This can lead to an upset stomach, acid reflux, chest pain, and ulcers in the long run. Moreover, you don't enjoy and appreciate the food you are eating.

There is also a widely held misconception that eating more frequently—instead of the regular three meals a day—will help reduce weight over time. *How can you lose weight by eating constantly?* In the '80s, grazing was thought to be an optimal way of losing weight. However, recent research does not support this belief. Controlled experiments show that there is no advantage to eating 12 smaller meals versus eating three or four meals per day, with the same total number of calories. Eating more often generally results in more food intake, and that will not likely make you lose weight.

What can we do about this?

The "French Connection"

Several studies[10] from the North American Association for the Study of Obesity found that *people who eat slowly eat less and feel more satisfied.* Unhurried eating allows ample time for the stomach to trigger the "I'm full" signal. The brain then realizes that you've had enough and commands your mouth to stop chewing. That "fullness" feeling translates into eating less. Which in a wider sense, feeds into the quality and amount of time we have left to live life to the fullest.

Let's look at how the French people eat, since in France, the obesity rate is just 11 percent compared to 37 percent in the U.S and 28 percent in the U.K. Only 40 percent of the French population is considered overweight, compared to 69 percent in the U.S. and 62 percent in the U.K. Well, guess what? The French are slow eaters. A study[11] from 2010 revealed that the French spend almost two and a half hours eating each and every day! That's because eating in France is considered a *pleasure,* and not just a basic body need. Lunch is the main meal of the day—and a great opportunity to socialize. The French *love* eating together—both with family and with work colleagues. Paris's Crédoc Institute reported that 80 percent of meals in France are taken with other people.

Based on data from nearly 60,000 people[10], researchers showed that eating slowly and cutting out after-dinner snacks result in lower obesity rates and smaller waistlines. Having a healthy weight is critical to a longer lifespan.

When you eat in the company of family and friends, you eat less because you are busy socializing. You are giving enough time for your stomach sensors to alert your brain to stop further intake when you are full. And more importantly, eating slowly enhances the pleasure of the eating experience. You *enjoy* the food and the time you spend consuming it— a great way to enhance the essence of your life.

If you follow this practice of pleasure-eating, you can indulge— without guilt—in a few bites of a delicious dessert without having to worry how many calories you just acquired. When you eat slowly, you will savor those bites by making every one count, and thereby deriving the same amount of pleasure as when you eat the whole dessert. You can have your cake and eat it too—but with less calories!

Typical portion sizes in France are also much smaller than their gigantic American counterparts. French food is famous for its small portions of extremely rich and delicious food. In France, quality is valued over quantity. That is why you will rarely find an all-you-can-eat deal in French restaurants. The approach over there is more all-you-*need*-to-eat. It's also why you won't like the look on the face of a French chef when you finish your meal and ask for a doggy bag. That's equivalent to an insult!

Consider too that it's also more difficult to enjoy the time spent eating when you are consuming your food "on the run" or in front of the TV or computer. Avoid eating on the move or while distracted—at work, driving, watching TV, or surfing the Internet—and savor the food by *slowing down.*

Three-and-a-Half More Years, Reclaimed and Savored

All those tips will improve your health—and greatly help your waistline. So, put on some music, light a few candles, invite a friend, family member, or colleague to sit down with you, and turn off the TV or any other distractions. Socialize *and* focus on your meal. You might actually be spending "more" time on eating, but that time will be more pleasant, and the benefits of your healthy eating can extend your lifespan as you reclaim more of your prized Life Essence.

Three and a half years is *nothing* to sneeze at. Keep on reclaiming—and you'll end up a centenarian!

Bonus Brain–Diet Material

For more details about the MIND diet, check the link below or click here to download your FREE copy of my eBook, *The Ultimate Guide to a Healthy Brain Diet*. Based on the well-tested MIND Diet, the book will give you an idea about some of the best brain superfoods that are essential for your brain's health.

https://dl.bookfunnel.com/nbc8yvihjv

Time Miracle Task

Over the next day, make a conscious effort to eat slowly and savor your meal.

Describe your experience:

_____

_____

_____

Did you end up eating less or more than usual?

_____

_____

_____

6

Body and Brain Exercise Hacks

Reclaim Up To 7 Years

⌒∞⌒

"The greatest wealth is health."

– Virgil

Break a Sweat

It's obvious that exercise is a key factor for a long and healthy life. Studies show that the habit of getting up and walking around for two minutes out of every hour can increase your lifespan *by up to 33 percent* (when started early on). One study[12] showed that walking for an hour a day can cut down the risk of getting stroke by as much as one-third. Another study followed the lives of 334,000 Europeans for 12 years and found that those who took daily 20-minute walks were 30 percent less likely to die prematurely than those who were inactive. The study concluded that 20-minute daily walks can add between 3 to 7 years to your lifespan.

The reason why this works is that when you're walking, you obviously can't be sitting. *Sitting for more than eight hours a day has been associated with diabetes, heart disease, and cancer.* Americans sit nine to ten hours on average each day, with some occupations going up to 12 hours. You can't expect to be healthy if you're living a sedentary lifestyle. The more you move around, the better, and it doesn't matter at what age you start: the benefits are immediate.

When you engage in physical activity, you burn calories—and that will help you control your weight. This also triggers anti-aging processes that prolong your life.

Exercise is also a great stress reducer. It stimulates brain chemicals that relax the body and make you happier. It will also make you feel better about your appearance, which in turn boosts your confidence and self-esteem; both of which add to your quality of life.

In the U.S., the average person walks around 5,000 steps each day. In the U.K., it's 3,000 to 4,000 steps each day. That's around 82,000 km or 51,000 miles in one lifetime. But the recommended goal is around 10,000 steps daily. That would be equivalent to *walking five times around the world over the course of a lifetime.* How can you achieve that?!

How to Walk Five Times Around the World

Simple. And it's realistic, too.

- **Don't use your car if you are within walking distance** from what you want to do.
- **Think about all the places nearby to which you can walk** and insert that transportation mode into your daily routine.
- **Use the stairs instead of elevators** and other lifts.
- **Get a fitness tracker** to keep track and find out how far you normally walk each day. The accumulating numbers will motivate you to walk more and reach your goal.

- **Start walking for 20 minutes daily.** If you do that from the age of 25 on, you will spend nine months walking over your lifetime. If you start at the age of 40, you will be walking for 6 months in your whole lifetime. That might seem a lot. But the benefits are a healthy lifestyle and 3 to 7 years added to your lifespan. You can also try combining walking with other beneficial activities. You can, for instance, listen to a podcast or an audiobook while walking and be able to finish two to three books a week.

In addition to the regular 20 minute daily walks, a good intense workout, 2 to 3 times a week, is highly recommended. One way to do that is to reconnect with the things you loved to do as a kid: riding a bicycle, playing softball, soccer, swimming, skiing, roller blading, tennis, etc. Exercise can be enjoyable, so resurrect one of your childhood fun activities and make that your regular exercise. It will give you a chance to unwind and enjoy the outdoors. It also fosters creativity. Aim for at least twenty minutes of moderate-intensity exercise.

Investing in your health is probably one of the most powerful ways to enhance the quality of your life and give you the ability to gracefully handle your daily stress. Exercise pumps up your endorphins—your brain's feel-good neurotransmitters. This is often referred to as a runner's high, but a quick nature hike can also produce the same feeling. It improves your mood and helps you relax.

You cannot avoid getting old, but you can delay it with daily physical exercise that will buy you more "Life Essence." Nine months of walking is a small investment compared to the seven years you add to your lifespan in return.

The Better Brain Workout

I've got to come out just and say it: a long life is worthless without a healthy brain to accompany it.

Yet one unavoidable fact of life is that our brains are going to deteriorate as we grow older. By now, haven't many of us experienced standing in a parking garage trying to remember where the he## we parked our darn car, or put our keys?

Well, maybe you weren't paying enough attention to where you parked in the first place. Or you didn't think about whether you popped those keys into your pocket or your purse. But as you grow older and such events occur more and more often, you start thinking, *maybe I'm losing my memory!*

As we age, our central nervous system becomes less sensitive, resulting in a slower brain-processing speed and a higher memory loss. We start noticing that it takes us longer to solve problems or make decisions than when we were younger. This is the result of wear-and-tear on all the axon wires that connect our brain regions together.

What can we do to keep our brains healthy so we remain as mentally fit as possible? Well, we already covered the basics of the MIND diet in the previous chapter 5. A diet that's good for your heart is also great for your brain. But here's some more better–brain advice:

- **Avoid brain "baddies."** That's right, no tobacco and no hangovers. Both smoking and excessive drinking have been linked to early dementia.

- **Get fit!** The fitter you are, the healthier your brain becomes. We already know how important regular exercise can be for our bodies—and our brain is a part of that. Physical exercise can nourish and stimulate our brain power. Studies show that people who exercise three times a week have a much lower risk of developing dementia.

- **Get enough sleep**. As we saw in Chapter 4, sleep is critical for a brain's health! It's so important for the formation of memories. Whatever you decide during the day to retain in your memory gets archived by your brain while you sleep. You know this already from how groggy you feel the next day when you've gone the previous night without sleep. Without enough quality sleep, you react slowly to new situations and have a limited attention span.

- **Socialize.** It provides a great brain workout! Join that book club; become part of a community or outdoor recreation group; or become a member of a sports team (within reason) at any age. All offer great ways to meet new people.

- **Stop living alone**. Social interaction stimulates our brain cells to grow new connections and creates new memories that will last for a long time. A study[13] done in Sweden found that people who lived alone and were single had a 60 percent increased risk of dementia! They were far more at risk than those who had close social ties or those who were married. If living with your family or spouse isn't an option for you, think about getting a compatible roommate.

- **Mentally challenge yourself.** You don't have to learn quantum physics, but you should engage in simple everyday activities like playing a musical instrument, playing cards, figuring out crosswords, and working on mentally engaging activities. The activity just needs to be a little mentally challenging so that you don't do it on autopilot.

A four-year study[14] that involved more than 5,000 dementia-free people over sixty-five years old in the French cities of Dijon and Montpellier found that those doing a crossword puzzle, playing cards, or practicing an artistic activity at least twice a week had a 50-percent reduced risk of developing dementia compared to those who did such activities less than once a week.

So, stretch your brain! Read that challenging book, take a new course, or try crossword puzzles or chess. Or, experiment with hobbies that require manual dexterity, such as painting or sculpting.

Shortcuts that Make Us Lazy

Modern life is all about making everything as efficient as possible. Think about it: every advance in technology offers the opportunity to do more things in less time with the least amount of physical and mental effort possible.

With smartphones, for instance, you don't just make calls; you take photos, play games, watch movies, interact on social media, listen to music, and communicate with laptops, TVs, and pretty much anything with a digital pulse. Unfortunately, these efficiencies are not great for your brain.

Take GPS or Waze, for instance. It's a great invention, especially if you have a bad sense of direction and get lost all the time. But after using it for a while, you start relying on it entirely—even for places you already know how to get to. Your brain gets lazy and, like so many things, if you don't use it you lose it. Stop relying on GPS or an app like Waze to get you somewhere; ask your memory or your good old-fashioned sense of direction (maybe even try to find a map!) to get you where you need to go.

Spell-check and autocorrect are other things that make it too easy to rely on a computer to catch your mistakes. As a result, no one really cares how to spell anymore (except those kids in the Scripps National Spelling Bee).

Technological shortcuts reduce your cognitive skills and hurt you in the long run. Sure, technology makes life easier and I'm not saying you should dump it completely—but don't rely on it entirely. Your brain needs exercise as well. If you stop practicing your problem-solving, navigation, and logical reasoning skills, your brain won't stay in shape. The time you spend on your brain workout is essential for a better quality of life.

Seven More Years—A No-Brainer

Efficiency is not your friend when it comes to maintaining a sharp brain; exercise is. *Keep strrrrrreching yourself;* in moving away from your comfort zone, you grow and develop new skills. In challenging yourself, you'll feel younger, act younger, and keep your brain healthy.

The combined effects of physical exercise, mental exercise, and a healthy brain diet will help add *as much as seven years* to your "Life Essence."

And that's a no-brainer!

Time Miracle Task

1. Over the next week, make a conscious effort to walk everywhere you can. Avoid using your car as much as practically possible.

Little by little this will become a habit.

2. Try out a few brain work-out tasks. Select one that you like and aim to perform it daily.

7

Work Time Hacks

Reclaim Up To 10 Years

∽∞∾

"Time is what we want most, but what we use worst."
– William Penn

Do What You Love

If you work the average 40-hour week from the time you complete your education until you retire at the age of 67—that's almost 50 years of employment—the total number of hours you will spend at work would be around 92,000 hours. That's equivalent to 10.5 years or 13.4 percent of your total time on this planet. It's the time you'll spend earning or attempting to earn money. If you are an office worker, statistics show that you'll spend around five years on average sitting behind a desk, four years talking on the phone, and two years attending meetings (by the way, these are not mutually exclusive).

For some people, work is something they love and enjoy spending time on. It's part of their life goal and dream. If you are one of those lucky people, great. You can immediately move those 10.5 years to your Life Essence account!

Wage Slaves

For most people, work is just a means to an end—a way to generate income to live a decent life. In that case, that time spent at work becomes a "time tax". It's not enjoyable nor memorable and does not add to life's overall satisfaction. The question is therefore, "How do I make my work time more pleasant and less of a curse?"

Let's face it, if you are lucky enough to have a job, there is a high probability you're not that excited to wake up and get to the office every morning. The latest statistics show that 70 percent of the employees in the U.S don't feel "engaged," according to a 2013 Gallup survey. They feel no real connection to their jobs. Most feel unappreciated and believe their work won't make a difference anyway.

One of the reasons for that unhappiness is because businesses evaluate employees by their productivity. The winners are those who can produce more and more in less and less time. Technology helps cause the wheels of time to turn ever faster and faster; we are able to fill our week with as many appointments and tasks as possible.

The reason behind our obsession with productivity is because we think time is money. This started with the Industrial Revolution, when clocks were used to measure labor—*and the value of time became associated with money*. That's why most people are paid by the hour.

Technology causes the wheels of time to turn increasingly fast. We fill our week with as many appointments and tasks as possible. Doing more things in less time makes us feel great. We start to falsely believe that if we just finish everything we have to do, we will be happy. But that time never comes, as we are constantly adding more things to do and more projects to work on. We are on the hamster wheel and running as fast as we can.

We feel miserable if and when we feel we need more time to finish things or start missing deadlines.

No matter how much money you make, your real wealth lies not in your bank account, but in how close you are to achieving your own dreams. If, **for instance, you sacrifice your time as a "wage slave" to an employer, you are working on someone else's plan while ignoring your own.** You become like excess butter on a slice of bread—and, unfortunately, that bread is not even your own. It is someone else's dream, agenda, or life goals on which you are stressfully working. There's a difference between doing work, and doing work that really matters. Sadly, we all have to spend time on busy-work that doesn't make much difference and that's a waste. If you're not sure, ask yourself this question: "*Will this matter in five years?*" It helps you differentiate between insignificant work that will consumes most of your time but not matter in a few years, and high impact work that will make a major change in your career, your life, in the lives of others.

Life in the Fast Lane

Once we equate time with money, we want to start making the most of it—and become obsessed with how to do more in less time. We allow ourselves to be swept away in a world that runs at a million miles an hour, and this affects our whole life. Becoming slaves to time —marinated in the culture of speed—has damaging effects on our health, relationships, and community.

A recent poll of more than 1,000 Americans found that nearly half felt they lacked enough time in daily life. "Time famine"—the feeling of having too much to do and not enough time to do it—is the cause of unnecessary stress and reduced performance.

Time pressure creates work-related stress that results in fatigue, heart problems, sleeping difficulties, anxiety, and depression. A survey titled "Life in the Fast Lane" found that 85 percent of adults living a hectic lifestyle suffer from indigestion and 62 per cent have a reduced interest in sex. Almost 80 percent admitted to excessive alcohol consumption. Their Life Essence years are likely to be grim and depressing.

Living the rat race changes your perspective on life: you become more impulsive, always looking for instant gratification. The smallest setback or slightest delay provokes fury. Even driving to work becomes an irritation. You start overtaking other cars because your mind is not here, but at your destination. But the car you overtook will catch up with you at the next traffic light—so you don't really gain much.

We were not designed for such a life. If you look back at the last 200,000 years of our evolution, we lived a life cycle that was adapted to the grand and slow pace of nature. It is only in the last 150 years that life started to speed up and has been accelerating exponentially with every new technology. Funny enough, these technologies were meant to *save us time so we could enjoy our life*... not to use that free time to do more things!

Technology also makes it easy for us to avoid person-to-person contact. You start spending more time on your email and less playing with your children or spending time with your wife. At work, you'd rather send an email to the colleague sitting across the office than to talk to him. It's "quicker" that way.

Time ≠ Money

Contrary to popular believe, time is not money. If you equate time with money, you will want to conserve it the way you treat money. So you'll be less eager to spend time on having fun, and more willing to work longer hours to make more money. The more valuable in monetary terms you perceive your time to be, the less eager you are willing to "waste it" on leisure. Relaxing at the pool becomes a waste of time. Having dinner with the family becomes a luxury that is hard to justify. Even when you manage to take some time off, it will be affected by the worry that you should be working. Do not deny yourself memorable moments for the sake of making more money.

The International Vacation Deprivation Survey has revealed that nearly one-third of Americans check work email or voicemail while vacationing. But researchers also have confirmed that people who are constantly "connected" to technology are generally more anxious and perceive time as running faster than usual. This leads to time starvation and the feeling that you are constantly running out of time. It takes away from your overall life satisfaction.

Every moment of the day, month, and year becomes a race to the finish line—a finish line, incidentally, that is never reached. Then you sit down one day—when twenty years have gone by—and you realize you failed to enjoy your life with all that running around. That's the last thing anyone wants.

Does Money^2 = Happiness?

Why the rush in the first place? What's so great about being in a hurry? Are you working frantically to make more money so that you reach a goal that will make you happy? When money is multiplied, does it result in more happiness?

Are you surprised to discover that a Gallup survey of 450,000 Americans, concluded that when people's annual income passes above

$75,000, they become more satisfied *but not happier*? There is a limit to how much happier more money makes us! The survey concluded that earning more than that income threshold does not contribute further to our emotional well-being.

Remember the Beatle's song, "Can't Buy Me Love"? Research has shown that people's happiness has remarkably little to do with how much money they have. Sure, money is great if it lifts you out of poverty. But beyond that, money cannot change your happiness levels by much. According to several studies, even winning the lottery gives only a short-term boost that doesn't last more than 18 months, after which it reverts back to its original level.

Ask yourself this: *how much time am I unnecessarily wasting on work that is not beneficial to my life fulfillment and emotional well-being? Am I making the most out of my life by earning more money?*

Instinctively, we think that more money, more food, more things, will make us happier. But you probably have far more now than you ever had in the past and you're probably not much happier. Moreover, do you really think anyone cares how much "stuff" you have? Will Smith puts it like that: "We spend money that we do not have, on things we do not need, to impress people who do not care." Sure, you might get a few "oohs" and "ahhs" when you show off your stuff, but do you really think people will regard you more highly because of that?

Having more money not the only ingredient for a good life. Friends and family, achievements, positive significance, and legacy are all equally important and you'll need to balance your time equally on each of these. You can't focus on one and ignore the others. It's a mistake to work on a job that you hate to make more money in the hopes of THEN having a family and THEN doing what makes you really happy. Life is too short for sequential gratification. Ralph Waldo Emerson wrote, "We are always getting ready to live but never living" and the late British Labor Party member Tony Benn once said, "People who sacrifice their life to reach the top leave no footprints in the sands of time." You don't want to be one of them.

A Change of Perspective

Here are a few things to consider that might convince you that it's time to change your perspective on how much you need to work:

- **Money has no true value except what we collectively ascribe to it.** Money is a man-made invention; but the time available for you to exist is not. Aside from helping us meet a basic standard of living, money is nothing but worthless pieces of paper that the government prints and declares valuable. In contrast, your time on this planet is real and infinitely priceless because you have a limited amount. Therefore, time does not equal money.

- **Working too much adversely affects your health.** Spending around four hours a day at a desk doubles your heart attack risk. Time on the computer increases your risk of vision loss by 40 percent, increases your insulin resistance (leading to diabetes), and affects your mental health. Remind yourself about the "French Connection" (page 71). French men and women make sure to relax, eat, and socialize every day… and their health only benefits as a result!

- **Working more than forty hours a week is *counterproductive.*** For this reason, the average working hours in countries all over the world—with the exception of North America—have been coming down! The residents of Norway, Denmark, Finland, and

Sweden— countries ranked among the top six most competitive nations—work, on average, thirty-five to thirty-seven hours per week. People in those countries report that, when they work less, their productivity increases and their quality of life improves.

Our brains are wired for about 3 to 5 hours of high-quality work each day—not 8. If used well, that's sufficient time to get the important things done.

The eight-hour work-day, a byproduct of the Industrial Revolution, maximized profitability, since making widgets on a factory's assembly line for eight straight hours was not too mentally challenging. But the Industrial Revolution ended a long time ago and with the advent of the Information Revolution, there is no added benefit now for employees to perform mentally challenging work for eight hours a day when their brain capacity for deep mental work is only three to five hours.

- **With only a limited amount of time to live, you can't afford to spend most of it just doing one thing at the expense of neglecting a whole lot of other things.** I'm sure many people have no choice but to devote their lives to work in order to make ends meet. But how many choose to live beyond their means, so they spend more of their lives working instead of enjoying life. All so they could have more "stuff." But there's more to life than just work and more work. Taking the kids to school, watching your son's baseball game, having a family supper, chatting with friends, starting a hobby, working on your dream passion—these are all equally important. You will only realize the cost of neglecting those when your kids are all grown up and you're left alone, or when a couple of decades fly by and you haven't started what you've always been passionate about.

Doing more is not the answer. Faster is not always better. You have a choice to make, and just because everyone else is running on that hamster wheel doesn't mean that it's the right thing to do. Slow down, that's what you need to do.

Slow-Down Work Hacks—with Great Results

When you slow down in your work life, you'll put quality before quantity. The quality of your projects will improve because you are not rushing what you are doing. You'll be thinking more clearly, meaning you are more likely to make better decisions and come up with better solutions to problems. Your creativity will naturally flow—and your new calmness will inspire your colleagues.

You'll start remembering what you did two days ago without having to look back at your planner. Your professional relationships will improve, because you'll be able to spare some time to focus on others. As you experience a new sense of camaraderie, accomplishment, and pride, your career becomes fun and fulfilling.

More importantly, you'll improve the quality of your life by reducing your stress levels. Modern companies, like Google and Apple, realize this already; they offer their employees more flexible work schedules, allowing employees to work at their own pace.

I know what you're wondering… How do I actually go about slowing doing and reducing the overtime I put in without jeopardizing my job or angering my boss? What steps can I take to achieve a slowdown that will improve the quality of my work rather than diminish it? And more importantly, how can I can convert the time spent at work to enjoyable time that can be added to my Life Essence years?

Here are some answers to those concerns:

- **Efficiently allocate your time to high-value work with the most impact.** Focus on what really matters. Set priorities in terms of your time and projects, getting rid of unimportant tasks and committing to avoiding time-wasting distractions.

- **Choose an endpoint to your workday.** If you stick to it, you'll ultimately end up improving your work efficiency! Psychologists refer to this as the "Vacation Paradox," which holds that you may never be able to finish all your work on a regular day, but a couple days before you go on vacation, you somehow manage to complete everything planned on that day in addition to that backlog of work that has been stacking up on your desk. This is only possible because when you have an endpoint to your workday, you will work more efficiently and get things done.

- **Pace yourself.** *The Economist* magazine recently wrote, "Forget frantic acceleration. Mastering the clock of business is about choosing when to be fast and when to be slow." Sure, there will be times when you have to rush to meet a deadline, but this cannot be a constant feature of your workdays. The trick is to know when to slow down and take your time and when to hurry.

- **Politely say, "No" to people.** (Something difficult for people pleasers and workaholics everywhere.) Recognize there are limits to your time/work commitments.

  Bringing home more work to do in your spare time, or constantly checking your email in the evening or over the weekend, will not help you achieve joy or satisfaction in life. By having a specific end to your workday or workweek, where you can disconnect and take your mind off work, you will be able to create time for all the other things you've always wanted to do but never had the time for. This can only happen when you know the limits of your time/work commitments and learn to politely say, "No." Work will be less frantic and more enjoyable when you have a good work–life balance and clear boundaries between your work and home life.

- **Say, "No" to yourself.** If work is your life and everything you do revolves around it, you'll become obsessed with doing more work in less time. You'll become a "workaholic productivity freak"—and you'll need to ask yourself, "Is that the best way to spend my limited precious time?" Stop taking on more work and learn to say "no" to curtail that unhealthy, unsatisfying tendency in yourself.

- **Make a work BFF.** According to a Gallup survey, one way workers find more meaning at work is when they have a best friend at the workplace. Work is not so much different from life in general—and what matters most in life are close social relationships. It is not about what you do, but rather who you are with.

  Socialize with your colleague within reason, of course. No need to become the office gossip or "chatterbox."

- **Discover where you are on the "job motivation scale"—then, move yourself over to the middle.**

  Start by asking yourself: what motivates me to do what I do? Is that an intrinsic or extrinsic motivation?

  "Intrinsic motivation" is when you do it because *you* want to—the motivation comes from within. "Extrinsic motivation" is when you do it just because you are getting something tangible out of it—a salary, a bonus, or the prestige, for example.

These two types of motivation make up the two extreme ends of a continuous scale. At the one end are those people who are motivated by tangible benefits (extrinsic). On the other end of the spectrum are those workers who are motivated by self-satisfaction.

If you lie at either extreme (all your motivators are tangible, or conversely, all your motivators are intrinsic), yours is *not* a healthy work motivation:

- If you work for just pure joy and without any external reward, you won't make much money and will last long at the job.

- If you work just for the money you earn, you won't be happy. This will make you more prone to stress when facing work challenges, and your work quality won't be as good if you derive no enjoyment from that which you do.

Achieving a good balance between the two types of motivation is best. If you have at *least one* intrinsically rewarding aspect to your job, it will help you get through stressful days.

- **Find time for idleness.** If your work relies on being creative, then you need a calm, unhurried, and stress-free day. Sitting at a desk staring at a computer screen will never result in creative breakthroughs. Creativity does not happen by working more, but by working less.

To come up with new concepts, you need to slow down, daydream a bit, and let go of rigid structures. You need to take time away from work, reflect, and then create. Take that nap (many companies offer power naps nowadays), enjoy that walk, read that book, and have that conversation. Some of the best ideas occur in the shower or when you're on vacation.

Several studies have shown that a certain degree of idleness is essential for producing the kind of mental state needed to connect concepts together and produce truly innovative ideas. Famous writers, like Charles Dickens, Victor Hugo, and J.R.R Tolkien, knew that all too well. They were known to take daily leisurely walks to help their creativity and productivity.

- **Delegate as deserved and needed, when that's possible.** If you constantly multi-task, you might be able to complete small jobs, but the big ones will remain open—and that increases the work pressure you feel. It is far better to seek help or delegate some of your responsibilities to reduce your workload instead of trying to do everything by yourself.

- **If you've tried everything and still cannot find joy in your work, try something new.** It is easy to get stuck, especially if you have been working for too long in a field that you may be good at but no longer enjoy. If your heart is no longer there, you should not assume that this is who you are and that is what you do. It is better to contemplate a change of career. By refocusing on your core abilities and the things you enjoy most, your work will feel like play. From Confucius's wisdom: "Choose a job you love, and you will never have to work a single day in your life."

Changing careers or jobs is certainly risky, especially in the state of the economy we live in. Without a doubt, you'll need to weigh the pros and cons to come up with wise decisions for you and/or your family. Still, since you only have one life to live, having the power to make positive changes in your life will make you happier.

Your ultimate goal is to convert the time you spend at work from being a "time tax" with the purpose of just earning money to being a part of your **Life Essence** and your life story.

Driving & Commuting

The time you spent driving or commuting back and forth to work can also be enhanced. One of the best ways I found to make this time memorable and beneficial is to start exploring different kinds of music while driving. It's incredible the number of amazing musical genres available for you to discover. These novel musical experiences will enrich you, both culturally and emotionally. You might also listen to nonfiction audiobooks in personal development, self-help, or skills improvement. You'll learn a lot of interesting things and that's a great benefit from the time spent commuting.

If you do that for half of the time you drive or commute, you will be able to convert at least 2 years of driving time into Life Essence time.

Time = Life = Ten Years Reclaimed

Remember, time is not money. **Time is life—and there is more to life than just work.** Nobody on their deathbed wished they spent more time in the office. Very rarely will someone be defining themselves by what they have achieved at work. After all, we come to this world with nothing, and we depart it in exactly the same way. Time spent earning money is unavoidable and as essential as those basic needs we saw earlier. By slowing down, creating intrinsic motivation, socializing, pacing yourself, delegating, and following the above tips, your work time will become more enjoyable and memorable. You will be able to reclaim those 10 years of work time from being a 'time tax' back into your Life Essence.

Time Miracle Task

List Some of the Intrinsic Motivations of Your Current Job.

1. _____
2. _____
3. _____

List Some of the Extrinsic Motivations of Your Current Job.

1. _____
2. _____
3. _____

Make A List of Things You Can Do to Have a Balanced Motivation (Extrinsic and Intrinsic).

1. _____
2. _____
3. _____
4. _____
5. _____

8

Unwiring Hacks

Reclaim 12 Years

∽

> "They put an off button on the TV for a reason. Turn it off."
> **– George W. Bush**

A Little Too Much?

In a sense, we are what we watch.

Most people watch TV to unwind or indulge in a new experience. Some watch TV to escape from their reality. We all watch programs that fit in with our needs. TV is great because, unlike reading or thinking, this kind of entertainment requires little to no effort. It is easily accessible and creates interest in life—especially when someone's life is boring. Sitting for hours on end absorbed in complicated storylines like *Game of Thrones*, *Breaking Bad*, or *House of Cards* has become some of our favorite after-work hobbies. A little bit of TV never hurt anyone, right?

Well, how much is a "little bit?" Netflix released data in 2016 that revealed it takes people just five days on average to finish a complete TV show season. The ATUS survey for 2016 showed that Americans spend 2.8 hours watching TV each day—accumulating to 80,486 hours in a lifetime!

That equates to **nine years** of an average life.

An even more alarming study conducted by Nielsen[15] found that the average American watches 34 hours of TV each week, or an average of five hours a day! And it gets worse the older you get; statistics show that people beyond the age of fifty watch around fifty hours of TV each week—around seven hours each day! In Europe, the average time spent watching TV is 3.7 hours a day—twelve years over the course of a lifetime.

You might think that's a lot and you would "never" watch that much, but I challenge you to calculate your own TV viewing time. Just write down all the shows you normally watch in a typical week and their duration. From sitcoms and dramas to reality shows, documentaries, and the news. Add in any full-length movies, shows on Netflix, Hulu, and Amazon Prime, and YouTube videos, and work out a rough estimate on how much time you spend on TV in a year and over a lifetime. **That is the amount of time you are actually "losing" out of your life.** While you might derive pleasure from watching TV, but it does not contribute to your life story. If you recall the last one or two decades of your life, TV time will not feature much in your memories. TV addiction is a waste time (and unhealthy as we shall see shortly) because its valuable time you could have spent socializing, entertaining, exercising, appreciating nature, enjoying a hobby, or fulfilling a dream.

Then you have to add the time spent surfing the Internet. We live in the digital age with emails and social media an integral part of our lives. But the prevalence of technology today is a double-edged sword. With a click of a button, you can access a tremendous amount of information on any subject you can imagine. With another click, you can end up wasting an hour of your day watching cats chasing balls or other equally silly things! There is no such thing anymore as a "quick" web search. It starts innocently enough when you want to search for a specific thing, but before you know it, you are 20 websites deep and one hour has been wasted on what was supposed to be a ten-minute search. Technology is supposed to save us time, but between emails and web-surfing, so much time ends up being wasted.

According to a study[16] by Mediakix, the average person will spend nearly two hours on social media every day, which translates to a total of five years and four months spent over a lifetime (adult years only). Whether it is YouTube, Facebook, Twitter, WhatsApp, Instagram, or Snapchat, we constantly check for updates on the latest happenings around us. Studies show the average person consumes more than 40 minutes of YouTube each day. This adds up to one year and ten months over a lifetime. Facebook comes next, with 35 minutes each day, which adds up to one year and seven months that Facebook-users will dedicate in a lifetime *to posting updates about their life instead of actually living it!* The total time spent on Snapchat is fourteen months; on Instagram, eight months.

For sure, many people use one or two social media apps and not all of them. But if you take an average of 1 year for social media, add the time spent watching TV and surfing the Internet, Nielsen[17] estimates Americans spend a total of 14 years of their life wired to some form of electronic media. No wonder we have little time to do anything else. That steals precious time away from other more meaningful things that actually make us happier. I am not saying that all social media and TV watching is bad. But just imagine what you can do if only a fraction of that time is spent on actually achieving your goals! Still not convinced? Let me give you a few reasons why TV is bad.

The Bad News about TV (and Other Media)

It is quite obvious that when you're watching TV, you're not doing anything else. There's a reason why TV addicts are called "couch potatoes": because TV watching is a very passive thing. Watching too much TV (or any kind of media) will eventually turn you into a potato. Worst still, a zombie!

You do not engage or interact; you just sit mesmerized and watch. Your brain activity slows down as if in a state of hypnosis. It is almost like you're sleeping, but you're not. You do not remember much of the TV shows you saw last week, in much the same way you hardly remember anything from your dreams. You live in a make-believe world while the real world passes you by. As a result, the nine years you'll spend watching TV and mindlessly surfing the net will disappear without leaving any memory trace in your mind. That time will never be part of your life story.

Here's more bad news about TV:

- **TV makes you fat.** It's bad for both your health and longevity. A recent study[18] from the University of Queensland, Australia showed that every hour you spend watching TV will shorten your life by 22 minutes! The researchers estimated that an adult watching six hours of TV each day can expect to live five years less than someone who does not. The reason is that excessive TV viewing results in a sedentary lifestyle and physical inactivity that provides greater opportunities for unhealthy eating and obesity. You tend to eat more while watching your favorite sitcom too. A study[19] from the Harvard School of Public Health showed excessive TV can increase the risk of causing obesity and type 2 diabetes.

- **TV is particularly bad for kids** Studies show that children who watch a lot of TV have *lower attention spans*. When a young child connects to the Internet, he can play a game, watch a cartoon, or even get answers for their homework. Children know they can rely on Google to get answers to a question, and so are likely to stop trying to figure things out for themselves. Steve Jobs, who pioneered some of the best home gadgets, was well known for not allowing his children to use an iPad.

  The kids also become *less patient*; a typical teenager will close a webpage that does not load within five seconds. This "on demand" instant gratification mindset will make it harder for them to cope with the real world. In fact, teens are among the worst addicts of social media—with the average teen now spending *up to nine hours each day on social platforms or surfing the net.*

  Surveys indicate that if our children consume around three hours of TV each week, they will have viewed around 16,000 murders and 150,000 acts of violence by the time they graduate from high school. Is that what we want them watching? Which leads me to…

- **TV messages are full of negativity—and when you expose yourself to all that negativity, you'll start seeing the world in a pessimistic way.** From comedies to drama to the news and reality TV, just about every TV show is negative. Comedies generally make fun of overweight, stupid, socially awkward, or racially stereotyped people. What's on the news? Usually stories of war, terrorist attacks, death, disasters, pain, and suffering. And dramas are, by definition, full of drama. TV shows with positive redeeming messages are quite the rarities these days. Is this how you want to be spending your precious time?

- **TV creates unrealistic expectations.** When you watch "beautiful people" on TV having a great time and doing amazing things and you compare that to your own life, you will feel inadequate and dissatisfied. As a result, your worldview is distorted, and your life feels empty when compared to the "perfect life" many live on TV. The essence of your time will seem dulled.

- **TV plays on your fears and drives you to buy.** Advertisers pay the TV networks and producers so you can watch their commercials and buy their things while sitting in front of the TV. You often end up buying the products not because you really need them, but because the subliminal messages in the ads play upon your fears and desires in a clever way that drives you to buy. Most ads are designed to show you how your life is lacking now and how you will be happier once you buy the product. So, you spend your money on something that you don't really need just to feel a short boost of happiness— which then quickly subsides back to the previous state of dissatisfaction.

Watching less TV and using less media will, in the long run, save you money that you can better use for some real relaxation and true happiness. It also will make you healthier and you'll live longer because you'll be moving around more.

But while it may seem easy to turn the power button on our remote controls off, it's not so easy to practice doing so as we live from day to day. Here are some motivational tips and hacks that can help you adhere to a routine of less TV and other media.

Tips for Tuning Out TV and "Smart" Media

- **Own a large library, not a large TV** (or, invest in an ebook reader.) Most successful people own large libraries—not large TVs. They know that our brains are amazing instruments that are constantly looking for new things to learn and they'd rather fill their brain with useful information from a good book than with junk from a trashy drama.

- **Consider what successful people do.** In *Rich Habits: The Daily Success Habits of Wealthy Individuals,* author Thomas Corley found that 70 percent of successful people do not watch more than an hour of TV a day. He also found that only 6 percent of them ever watch reality shows compared to 78 percent of poor people.

  Successful people look at time as an investment rather than an expense. They invest their time in actions that take them closer to their goals. They realize that spending an hour watching TV rather than spending it on your passions or dreams is time that's gone forever and can never be recovered. Instead, 86 percent of successful people enjoy reading at least thirty minutes each day. They find reading to be much more relaxing and entertaining than watching TV.

- **Hide the dangerous time-sucker!** Stick the remote inside a cabinet, or place something over it so that you and your kids don't immediately spy it when you get home from school or work.

- **Leave the house,** returning only after that urge to watch the TV has subsided. Go take the dog on a walk; do a quick errand; or relax in a warm bath surrounded by scented candles.

- When everything else fails and you cannot help yourself but watch

TV, **give yourself a limit on how much time you are willing to waste on TV.** Gradually decrease that amount until you "flush" TV-watching out of your system.

- If you really enjoy watching TV for a short time to de-stress after your workday, **how about making it a family-time activity only?** You could have all family members agree on a certain amount of TV time, which is watched together as a family and is a previously agreed-upon program or movie. Some TV show choices cold be educational like a documentary, biography/memoir, DIY show; or myth-busters show. These have some redeeming value.

Time to Unplug

I know you love your smartphone. We all do. We take them everywhere we go, while traveling, eating, sleeping, attending meetings, and even to those toilet visits. The average person checks their phone 150 times a day. Your son is addicted to video games? Your daughter obsessed with "like" on Instagram? Can't blame them. Social media is carefully designed to keep them coming back for more. App notifications, "likes," emails, and messages that self-destruct compel us to keep checking so that we're not missing something really important. The result is 'technology addiction' that's a waste of our precious time.

I am not saying you should abstain from technology because that is impossible in this day and age. What I am proposing is that you unplug and avoid being perpetually addicted and connected to technology. Here are a few ways you can do that:

- **Learn to prioritize.** When having lunch or talking with someone, avoid checking your phone. Keep it aside, focus on your lunch, enjoy that conversation, and give priority to what is more important. The world won't stop if you do.

- **Keep your phone away from your bed.** Do you check your phone first thing when you wake up? Check Facebook notifications before you sleep? You never know what you'll get. It's like slot-machine addiction. People keep pulling the lever to get a reward. But putting your device on silent and far away from your bed avoids the temptation to check it before you sleep or when you wake up.

- **Turn-Off App notifications.** Make a habit of checking your smartphone at certain set times. Schedule a timer to go off at a certain time every day to check your feeds.

- **Limit the amount of social media postings.** Do you really seriously believe anyone cares how you're feeling at this particular moment, or where you checked-in, or having an expensive dinner at a fancy restaurant? It makes you feel good, but trust me, no one cares.

Twelve Years, Reclaimed!

If you reduce your TV viewing and social media usage from 5 hours to just 1 hour a day, it adds up over your remaining years and you will be able to reclaim at least 12 years back into your life. You can then use that time to hang out with friends, spend time with family, read books, invest in yourself, exercise, and start new hobbies.

Sure, TV can *seem* relaxing after a long day's work, but these other activities are actually more relaxing and rewarding—and will better impact your life with health, fulfillment, and happiness. You only live once and there are far too many more important things to do than wasting your precious time in front of a hypnotizing box or screen. Minimize media consumption and start living instead.

Time Miracle Task

Make a decision to limit TV and media consumption to 1 hour or better not to watch TV or use any screens for a day. Next Try it for a week.
Make a note of all the things you did instead:

1. _____
2. _____
3. _____
4. _____
5. _____

Which of these things were more meaningful than watching TV?

1. _____
2. _____
3. _____
4. _____
5. _____

9

Your Average Day Optimized

❧

"Life is no brief candle for me. It is sort of a splendid torch
which I got hold of for the moment and I want to make it
burn as brightly as possible before handing it on to future
generations."
– Bernard Shaw

Better With or Without?

We have covered some of the hacks you can use to maximize your Life Essence years by optimizing the time spent on sleeping, eating, exercise, work, and media. What follows is a simple comparison of a typical weekday for an average person, before and after these "quality hacks" are implemented.

This will give you an idea of how much real time we can save each and every day—and add to our time winnings.

The Average American Typical Weekday—Pre-Hacks

You wake up to an earsplitting alarm for the start of another workday. You're exhausted because you stayed up past midnight the night before—perhaps to catch up on some work or check Facebook.

You hit the snooze button a few times before you finally get up. Now you're already running late, with no time for breakfast.

You reach the office and settle into your typical work routine: sitting for hours; you check your emails, the news, and social media; and drink a cup of joe. It's almost noon, and you haven't accomplished anything yet. To catch up, you decide to work through lunch, and order something to eat at your desk.

Despite doing this, you still don't get any real work done.

As the day progresses, your energy level drops. By three p.m., it's time for another cup of coffee to reignite you. Now you really start working on the most important tasks of the day, and though you make partial progress, it's not enough. The day is over, and you haven't met some of your deadlines. You decide to stay late at the office.

You end up missing dinner, and by the time you get home, the kids are about to go to bed. You enjoy some leftovers while watching TV and checking social media or more emails—and the daily grind repeats itself the next day.

If this routine mirrors yours, you are mostly spending your day on "time tax" activities. There is little time to really enjoy life or achieve any goals.

In the long run, such an unhealthy lifestyle will cut a few years from your lifespan! It's non-productive, and nothing worthy gets done. Life simply is passing you by.

Let's compare that to another weekday that's optimized with time hacks that minimizes time taxes and maximizes Life Essence.

The Average American Optimized Weekday—Post-Hacks

After going through your nighttime ritual—*no TV or screens allowed*—you hit the pillow at 11:00 p.m. Before you go to sleep, you jot down the three most important things you want to achieve the next day, and quietly request your subconscious to work on a particular issue or challenge as you slumber.

After a good six-and-a-half hours of high-quality sleep, you wake up at 5:30 fully energized. You go through a "thought-dump" process to harvest the solutions your subconscious mind came up with during the night. There is plenty of time for a light, healthy breakfast that you enjoy with your family. With an hour and a half added to your day, you can afford to work a bit on your passion/hobby, focus on learning a new skill, or do a quick work out.

While driving or commuting to your workplace, you listen to a self-help or education audiobook and learn something new. You do that around half of the time you drive/commute, and you convert 2 years out of the 4 years that's normally spent driving/commuting into Life Essence years.

At the office—before you get stuck reading through emails—you start with the most challenging work tasks first. Your motivation is high, and you love what you do.

You plan to work in ninety-minute chunks, followed by fifteen-minute breaks, throughout your workday.

Having accomplished a lot by morning's end, you get away from your desk to enjoy a nice healthy lunch out with some colleagues or friends. There is even some time for a fifteen-minute walk.

Once you are back in the office, you use your afternoon for scheduled meetings, checking emails, and clearing your inbox. Before you leave for the day, you put together a plan for the next day, prioritizing important goals and necessary tasks.

At home, it's time for a 20-minute workout or walk, followed by dinner with your family. After some meaningful conversations, you devote some time to work more on your passion projects. Even if you have a TV, you will still have time for your hobbies because you limit TV watching to one hour a day. Afterwards, you make sure to stay away from "screen time," and you read a book or write in your diary before you go to sleep.

Here are the gains you'll accumulate from your optimized day:

1. You'll reclaim at least an hour and a half each morning. This adds **three years** to your Life Essence.

2. You've converted the **three-and-a-half years** you normally spend eating over a lifetime into a healthy and socially enjoyable experience. So you can add that onto to your Life Essence as well.

3. **Two years** of driving and commuting time are enhanced from being just traveling time to useful learning time that furthers your goals and dreams.

4. The workday was productive at the office, and you're satisfied with what you did. The **ten years** that you'll normally spend earning money became enjoyable and gratifying and can be added to your Life Essence account.

5. Having reduced TV viewing and media consumption time, you'll gain at least **twelve more years** for far more enjoyable things.

6. Your twenty minutes of daily exercise, along with your healthier diet, adds up to **seven more years** to your overall lifespan.

Fifty Percent of Your Life, Freed Up

By ingeniously using the time we spend caring for our bodies, sleeping, eating, driving, and working, as well as moderately engaging with media consumption, we can rethink up to 31 years of our life and convert them towards the more satisfying Life Essence Years. On top of that, you can add up to 7 years to your life by following a healthy diet and exercising regularly. The total time gained results in approximately 38 years of Life Essence that's now available for you to live and enjoy your life.

You just freed up 50 percent of your life!!

Happiness in life comes from the gratifying feeling that your time is well spent. In the following table, you can calculate your own time optimization and estimate how many "time tax" years you can reclaim. Any time you free up can be used to improve your overall life satisfaction. You can then act like the miracle you are and go on to enjoy and make the most of it

The following table will help you plan your own time optimization based on what you have learned so far. In the next section (Part 3), I go over what makes us happy and provides meaning to our life, as this is essential to our Life Essence years. Part 4 will cover a few helpful ideas to enrich those Life Essence years.

Time Utilization Comparison

Time Category	Before Optimization		After Optimization	
	Hours Spent Each Day	Years Spent From Remaining Years	Hours Spent Each Day	Years Spent From Remaining Years
Basic Needs				
Sleeping				
Eating				
Grooming				
Shopping				
Housework				
Exercise				
Earning Money				
Education and Work				
Driving				
Media Consumption				
Time spent on TV				
Time spent on Social Media and the Internet				
Total Years Spent				

PART 3

HAPPINESS & MEANING

10

Lessons from the Convent

You Don't Have to Become a Nun to Live Longer

"Very little is needed to make a happy life; it is all within yourself, in your way of thinking."
– Marcus Aurelius (Roman Soldier A.D. 120)

An interesting clue to a long and happy life comes from the Convent of the School Sisters of Notre Dame—through what is famously known as the Nun Study[20].

In 1986, neurologist Dr. David Snowden made a 30-year partnership with the convent nuns to observe and test them in an effort to answer the question about who gets Alzheimer's disease and why. The great thing about studying nuns is that many of the variables were controlled because the nuns lived communally in their convent. So, none of them drank, smoked, had sex, got married, or had any kids.

For years, the research team analyzed the nuns' genes, testing them on how many words they could remember minutes after reading flashcards. They measured them on their strength and balance. Once each nun from the study died, the scientists removed her brain and shipped it to a laboratory for analysis.

One day, the researchers discovered a pile of cardboard boxes full of handwritten autobiographies written by the nuns when they were in their twenties, back when they first joined the convent and took vows. The autobiographies contained a high level of emotional content that indicated the nuns' happiness levels at the time of writing.

The researchers were able to categorize the autobiographies, along with the nuns who authored them, into positive, negative, or neutral "levels of happiness." They then compared the nuns' early outlook on life against how long they lived. What they found was staggering:

- Nuns who were happiest in their twenties lived ten years longer than those who were least happy.

- By age eighty, the most cheerful group had only lost 25 percent of its population, while the least cheerful group had lost 60 percent.

- Fifty-four percent of the happiest nuns lived to the age of 94 while only 15 percent of the least happy reached that age.

Similar findings have been confirmed by various other researchers. As part of the English Longitudinal Study of Ageing[21], researchers collected data from 9,300 men and women aged 50 and older and measured how happy they were. The participants had to record their levels of happiness and anxiety at four specific times each day for a period of five years.

Ten years later, the researchers found that those who tended to be happier were 35 percent less likely to die than their gloomier counterparts. Those who said they did not enjoy their lives at any time were the most likely to die.

A similar study that followed 5,000 students for more than 40 years found that those who were most pessimistic as students tended to die younger than their peers. The research showed that good moods are correlated with long life.

The conclusion is clear: how happy you are today determines how long you're going to live. That's because enjoying life is known to reduce stress, which in turn improves the immune system and prolongs life. If you really want to live longer, you might want to make your own happiness a priority.

Being diligent about exercising, eating healthy, and getting enough sleep is great for life longevity. But as the Nun Study[20] showed, your own happiness is equally important and cannot be neglected.

Clearly you don't have to become a nun to live longer. However, having a positive outlook can add several years to your Life Essence. By being happy, you don't just enjoy those lifetime-essence years; you actually prolong them as well.

Now, how can *you* be happy?

11

How to Be Happy

The Three Habits of Happiness

∽∞∼

"The happiness of your life depends upon the quality of your thoughts."
– Marcus Aurelius (Roman Soldier A.D. 120)

Your Happiness Set-Point

We tend to evaluate the quality of our life primarily by how happy we are. But what makes us happy has been the subject of many theories. The most popular is arguably the Set-Point Theory.

The Set-Point Theory maintains that our level of happiness is a somewhat constant personality trait, and that we cannot change our happiness levels by much. Accordingly, happy experiences can only offer a brief lift or boost to our mood that eventually fades away as we return to our inherent happiness set-point.

This finding is supported by a famous study[22] on lottery winners that goes back to 1978, when researchers from the University of Massachusetts interviewed lottery winners and compared their answers with people who had suffered a terrible accident that left them paraplegic. The study found that the happiness levels of lottery winners was boosted by the win—but that the new happiness level did not last long and returned to its pre-winning level after just a few months. In many cases, the accident victims were actually slightly happier after the incident compared to the lottery winners once their happiness boost subsided!

The study concluded that **people generally have a set-point of happiness that they tend to return to, even after life-changing events.** Psychologists call this the "hedonic treadmill," which is the human tendency to return to the individual's routine happiness level despite the occurrence of positive or negative events.

Our happiness set-point is preprogrammed into our genes—although is it also shaped by our environment. Still, scientists suggest that as much 50 percent of our happiness is dictated by genes. Some people are born with a natural disposition to be happy, while others are born with a tendency towards being gloomy. Each one of us has a unique happiness set-point.

Another 10 percent of our happiness is due to external events; when we buy our dream car, find our partner, take that dream vacation, or get a pay raise, we get a 10-percent boost to our happiness level. These events make us happier—but only temporarily. Recall how the positive effects of a vacation do not last very long, with most of us normally returning to our pre-vacation happiness levels within two to three weeks.

The remaining 40 percent of what makes us happy **is inside our mind and under our control.**

This is what we can actively change.

Happiness is a Choice

As the Greek Stoic philosopher Epictetus once said, "It's not what happens to you, but how you react." Shakespeare weighed in with these words: "There is nothing either good or bad but thinking makes it so."

It's up to *you* to interpret what happens to you in a positive light.

Anti-apartheid revolutionary and political leader Nelson Mandela was imprisoned for twenty-seven years, and he became famous partly for choosing not to have any resentment against the apartheid regime. He viewed his time in prison as a "holiday," during which he had time to reflect, learn, and even write his autobiography.

By controlling your attitude, you'll be at least 40 percent happier. Thousands of self-help books tackle the subject of happiness and ways to achieve it, but in my opinion, they all boil down to a few "tried-and-true" habits.

The Three Habits of Happiness

Happiness Habit #1: Exercise and Maintain Your Physical Well-Being

We saw earlier that regular exercise can add up to seven years to your lifespan (Chapter 6). Recent studies have also shown that people who exercise regularly are also happier. The popular adage, "sound body, sound mind," is very true.

Exercise reduces stress and releases endorphins into your body that create a kind of euphoria and are addictive over time. Many people refer to that as "runner's high."

It really doesn't matter what particular activity you chose. Just make it a regular habit of yours to work up a sweat… and get the full happiness benefits.

Happiness Habit #2: Form and Nurture Your Close Relationships

People who have one or more close friendships are happier, as loneliness often leads to depression. True friends are really worth their weight in gold.

Still, it's not easy these days to know who our "true friends" are. We put much value on fun, but not enough on loyalty. We all have fair-weather friends who are there only when times are good but **having a true friend—someone whom you know you can rely on in times of need—is a real treasure.**

A true friend is the one who offers to bring you over some chicken soup when you're sick. They're the one you call when you've been dumped by your significant other. They're the one who calls you when you've been working too hard and haven't had a break. They're the first one you think of when you want to enjoy a lunch out

Friends improve the quality of our life. A vacation with good friends is better than taking one alone. Working with great friends is better than working with rivals.

A variety of studies confirms that **having five close relationships seems to be optimal.** But don't take those relationships for granted, ever; it's important to put effort into them! Even the best friendships "thaw" over time and need to be continuously nurtured. And what matters most to keeping the bonds alive is *how often you share your personal feelings with your friend.*

Every time you connect with a friend, you strengthen your bonds with them AND boost your happiness levels. Studies show that people deprived of friends or close family can end up depressed. Therefore, taking steps to stay close to your extended kin and buds will make you happier.

Emails, telephone, and video calls can now easily be used to that end when physical proximity is not possible. This is a lot easier than in the old days, when a family member moved away and we had only the phone (with its long-distance charges) and an occasional visit to keep the relationship alive.

Now when someone moves away, you can Skype or FaceTime them and get a video of your friend's face as you chat.... It's like having them with you.

Even better than socializing with your friends is... being in love. Studies have consistently shown that **people with partners often are significantly happier than single people.** With ordinary friends, you cannot share whatever comes to your mind. Much of your inner dialogue is either too trivial or too intense to be of interest to this kind of friend. But in the company of a lover, you are pretty much granted unlimited care, attention, and concern. You are accepted as you are, more or less. So, you are able to reveal your extreme vulnerabilities and innermost thoughts—and still survive! This kind of free access is crucial to a happy life.

The time you spend socializing and in love-related activities is priceless. Friends and family make life worth living. Therefore, spending time with people you love forms the pillar of a purposeful and happy life.

Happiness Habit #3: Be Kind

Kind people are happy—and happy people are kind. Countless studies have confirmed that generosity is linked to greater life satisfaction. Volunteering to do charity work or simply caring for others will make you happier and less depressed. Service to others could take very simple forms: holding the door open for someone, doing chores for other people, donating to charity, and/or buying lunch or a card for a friend.

Random acts of kindness make you optimistic, and positive. They also create emotional warmth, which releases your body's oxytocin, occasionally referred to as the "love hormone." This reduces blood pressure and protects the heart, thus helping prolong your life.

There is even evidence that caring for others can permanently boost your happiness set-point beyond that which you inherited through your genes! The reason is that the more value you create for others, the more value you assign to yourself.

Helping others also enhances your self-esteem and sense of purpose— and that will make you a happier person.

Kindness is contagious! Those who witness or benefit from an act of kindness are more likely to be kind themselves. One single act of kindness can spread through your social surrounding and may return back to you. The 'paying it forward' movement displays this concept best. Doing something nice for someone is not an act that needs to be repaid, but rather should be shared with someone else to create a lasting ripple effect. So if someone thanks you for your generosity, ask them kindly to "pay it forward."

What goes around comes around: helping others is essentially helping yourself!

Lows and Highs

A cautionary bit of advice…

We all want to be happy, successful, healthy, wealthy, and loved. But if you think that these are "owed" to you, you will feel miserable when you don't get them.

Are you unhappy because you think you deserve success? Well, then ask yourself: did I do all I can to warrant it?

Do you feel down because you think you deserve a great relationship? Well, then ask yourself: how well am I treating people? How much am I working to improve myself in the eyes of other people?

Your desire to be happy cannot be fulfilled without a significant

investment of effort. The things that are most challenging are often the things that prove to be most rewarding. Happiness requires hard work.

And remember too that being happy every hour of every day is *not* possible. Failure and pain are life's greatest teachers. You'll learn much about yourself in times of struggle. Sometimes, you need to experience life's sorrows and low points to be able to appreciate the things that truly make you happy.

Time Miracle Task

Complete the Happiness Level Quiz by clicking the link below OR answering the following questions.

https://goo.gl/forms/5crX7ONIdPBwkUN53

Figure Out Your Current Happiness Level

Below is a quick quiz that can measure how happy you are now compared to the rest of the world. Circle the answer that best describes you. Please take the test and do not just read over it, otherwise your score will be skewed. Answer honestly for a realistic score.

1. How often do you share your feelings with friends or relatives?
   a. Never
   b. Once or twice a month
   c. Once or twice a week
   d. Three times a week or more

2. How often do you do kind things for others?
   a. Never
   b. Once or twice a month
   c. Once or twice a week
   d. Three times a week or more

3. How much time do you spend on social media per day?
   a. Less than 2 hours
   b. 2 to 4 hours
   c. 4 to 6 hours
   d. 6 to 8 hours

4. How often do you do at least 20 minutes of physical exercise?

   a. Never

   b. Once or twice a month

   c. Once or twice a week

   d. Three times a week or more

5. I find a deep sense of fulfilment in my life by using my strengths and skills towards a purpose greater than myself.

   a. Never

   b. Rarely

   c. Sometimes

   d. Often

6. I engage in activities or hobbies (sports, writing, etc.) that I find challenging and absorbing.

   a. Never

   b. Once or twice a month

   c. Once or twice a week

   d. Three times a week or more

7. I have feelings of gratitude towards people and events from my past.

   a. I never feel this way.

   b. I rarely feel this way.

   c. I sometimes feel this way.

   d. I often feel this way.

8. I am able to focus on the present moment and do not get distracted by thoughts of the past or future.
   a. I never feel this way.
   b. I rarely feel this way.
   c. I sometimes feel this way.
   d. I often feel this way.

9. I am optimistic about the future.
   a. I never feel this way.
   b. I rarely feel this way.
   c. I sometimes feel this way.
   d. I often feel this way.

10. I feel that my life is meaningful (i.e., has an important quality or purpose).
   a. I never feel this way.
   b. I rarely feel this way.
   c. I sometimes feel this way.
   d. I often feel this way.

Time to calculate your happiness score!
   - For every (a) answer, give yourself 1 point.
   - For every (b) answer, give yourself 2 points.
   - For every (c) answer, give yourself 3 points.
   - For every (d) answer, give yourself 4 points.

Add up the points from each of the questions above and calculate the total score.

Time Miracle Task

What Is Your Happiness Score? _____

1. If your happiness score is between 10 and 19, you are below average and tend to be unhappy. There is room for improvement. Keep reading.
2. If your happiness score is between 20 and 29, you are generally happy.
3. If your happiness score is between 30 and 40, that's great! You are above the average and tend to be a very happy person.

12

Lessons From the Blue Zones

Finding Ikigais!

∞

"He who has a why to live can bear almost any how."
– **Friedrich Nietzsche**

"Without a goal, you can't score."
– **Unknown**

In the Land of the Immortals

In the early 1970s, *National Geographic* began a study[23] to identify areas on the globe called "blue zones" where people live longer, healthier, and more active lives than the rest of the world. Five zones were identified: Okinawa (Japan); Sardinia (Italy); Nicoya (Costa Rica); Icaria (Greece) and among the Seventh-day Adventists in Loma Linda, California. The most intriguing of those locations is the small island of Okinawa in Japan. The percentage of people aged more than one hundred years in Okinawa is the highest in the world, and the average lifespan is 84 for men and 90 for women. Ancient Chinese legends refer to Okinawa as the "land of the immortals." Centenarians in Okinawa are known for their health and vigor; they do not suffer from heart disease or Alzheimer's. Undoubtedly, there is a lot we can learn from the Okinawa culture, and what makes Okinawans live that long, healthy life.

Okinawans don't overeat. They practice something called "hara hachi bu," which is the method of eating until they are 80 percent full. They never eat till they are stuffed. Their daily caloric intake is far lower than ours—around 1,800 calories, compared to a typical Western daily calorie count of 3,700. Okinawans even use smaller plates for that purpose.

In addition to that, their diet is also very similar to the MIND diet that we explored in Chapter 5 in more detail: high on fruits and vegetables, low on salt, and foods containing plenty of fiber and antioxidants that protect against cancer and heart attacks. On average they eat three servings of fish a week, soy products like tofu, Kombu seaweed, sweet potato, turmeric, jasmine tea, and the local bitter cucumber "goya."

Scientists from the U.S. National Institutes of Health and Japan's Ministry of Health have been following Okinawans since 1976. In the Okinawa Centenarian Study (OCS)[24], they found that the secrets to longevity among those of advanced age were mainly diet and, more importantly, a concept called, *ikigai*—pronounced "ee-kee-guy." *Ikigai* can be roughly translated to mean, "the reason that I get up in the morning." It is very similar to the positive attitude we already saw in the Nun Study. **Everyone in Okinawa has at least one *ikigai*.**

Pursue Passionate Purposes

Ikigai is something you look forward to doing, or a purpose about which you are passionate. You find a thing that you enjoy and find emotionally energizing. Here, it's **all about the journey, and not the destination.** You may have multiple *ikigai(s)*, which may change over time. What matters is that they are meaningful and inspiring to *you*.

To test the effect of having an *ikigai* on longevity, a group of Japanese scientists from the Tohoku University Graduate School of Medicine spent seven years studying the longevity of 43,000 Japanese adults[25]. They looked at their age, gender, education level, weight, cigarette and alcohol consumption, exercise, stress levels, and whether they had an *ikigai* in their life. What they found was that participants who had an *ikigai* were more likely to be happy, married, educated, and employed. At the end of the seven-year study, 95 percent of the participants with an *ikigai* were alive.

Sadly, most people struggle to find their *ikigai(s)*. Modern life feels like a rat race when you're running daily on a treadmill that's not moving you anywhere. You work, go home, sleep, rinse, and repeat. You may dread those five weekdays and look forward to recharging on the weekends. You anticipate retirement in the hope that you will be able to "start living" then. But when retirement comes, there is no purpose attached to it, because the previous 40 years of your life had no *ikigai(s)*. Today, the average retiree has on average fifteen years of retirement—and that's a long time to go without a purpose in life. We've all heard anecdotal stories about people who retired and died shortly thereafter. This also explains why depression and addiction are quite common among senior citizens.

But it's never too late to create meaning. The conclusion from the Okinawa Centenarian Study is that **having "reasons to wake up in the morning" and purpose to life are crucial for prolonging life.**

Now that we know what *ikigai(s)* are, in the next chapter we will explore way to define yours.

Time Miracle Task

Brainstorm what your *Ikigai* might be.

List the top 5 reasons why you wake up in the morning.

1. _____

2. _____

3. _____

4. _____

5. _____

Don't worry if you can't figure this all out. The next chapter will give you some ideas to consider that will help you define your ikigai.

13

Find Your Passions

Create Meaning

❦

"The two greatest days of your life are the day you were born
and the day you find out why."
– Mark Twain

Questions that Go to the Gut

How do you make the most of your time? Let's tap into your intuition… what is it that you truly want to be, deep down in your gut? What are you passionate about in life? But by that, I don't mean finding your "one and only" life's purpose. No, **do what the residents of Okinawa did by asking yourself:** what are the important things I can do with my time? What are my life's passions?

No one but you can answer that question. You—yes you, and only you— are the one who is going to create meaning for your life's story. You are going to "own" your life.

By finding your passions, you start living a passionate life.

Let's get you started. Here are three questions to help you identify the important and meaningful things in *your* life.

Question #1: What Makes the Whole World Disappear for Me?

Have you ever experienced a time in your life when you were so absorbed in what you were doing that the rest of the world seemed to have disappeared? A situation where you were totally focused on an activity… so much so that you were not even aware of yourself? When it was as if time ceased to exist, and only when you were done did you realize how much time had actually passed?

If you answered yes to the questions I just posed, then you have experienced the state of consciousness that psychologists call "flow."

During a flow experience," the actions you perform are effortless and stand out as exceptional moments in life. You feel that things are exactly as you want them to be and cannot be any better. The experience in such moments is intense if held against the unexciting backdrop of our daily routines and tasks. **Any activity that puts you into a state of flow should be on your list of things that are important in your life.**

People describe such flow experiences with other expressions, like "being in the groove," or, "getting lost in the book." During these times, they simply "forget about themselves."

Athletes may use the term "being in the zone." Artists describe "aesthetic raptures," or a "heightened state of consciousness." Religious mystics refer to their experience of this time as being in "a state of ecstasy" (and we're not talking about the drug).

Many famous thinkers, artists, and sports figures were known to perform only when in a state of flow. During that time, they are likely to forget about some of their basic needs!

When Isaac Newton was working on his gravitational theory, his mother had to regularly remind him to eat because he became so absorbed in his work that he would forget to eat for entire days. Historical sources suggest that Michelangelo may have painted the ceiling of the Vatican's Sistine Chapel while in such a mental state. Some say he painted for days at a time and was so absorbed by his work that he lost track of time. He did not eat or sleep, going until he passed out. He would then wake up re-energized and start to paint again in a state of complete absorption.

Formula One world champion, Ayrton Senna, once famously described his flow experience while driving his McLaren: "I was going faster and faster… and I suddenly realized that I was no longer driving the car consciously."

So, ask your heart, "What do I love to do?"

By doing what you love you will be happy and inspired.

If your life is devoid of passion, you will never feel like you are living the life you were meant to live. Living a life pursuing the things you are passionate about—the things that get you into the flow—is the way to live a happy life.

Question #2: What is My Contribution to Saving the World?

If you watch the news on any day, you will notice that the world has a few problems. By "few," I mean, "The whole planet is one big mess, and we are probably all going to die!"

Ask yourself, "Which problem is dear to my heart?" Climate change, religious conflicts, poverty, poor education, government corruption, domestic violence, or mental health care (to name a few)?

Then, how can you use your precious time to contribute, even in a tiny way, to making the world a better place? How can you ease the suffering of others?

Pick a problem that you care about and start "saving the world."

When you take your unique strengths and use them for a purpose

that is greater than yourself, you start contributing to making a difference—and you live a meaningful and happy life.

As you do so, you may choose to join a group of people who have similar concerns and contribute to making this world a better place.

Several studies have found that what goes through the minds of people on their deathbeds is not fast cars or more money, but their lasting impact on this world. So… is the world a better place because you are here, or not?

Those who contribute the most are more likely to die with a smile on their face.

Question #3: What Would I Do if I Had Only One Year to Live?

This question, surprisingly, has many practical benefits. It allows us to focus on the important things in our life.

If you had one day or one year to live, how would you use it? Would you still do some of the things you consider important now, or would they become insignificant? Would you consider spending more of those precious moments with the people dear to you, and less with the people with whom you are now spending your time?

These kinds of questions force you to think about your priorities. The key point is not about that one year—for you almost certainly have more than one year to live—it's more about the finality of your own time.

We all hope to live a long, healthy, happy, and meaningful life. Nobody wants to die. Even those who believe in Heaven don't want to die to get there. As Ernest Hemingway would say, "Every day above Earth is a good day."

But death is not optional. From the moment we are born, we're thrown on a rollercoaster ride that's leading us to the only certain event in life: death. That reality is mentally and emotionally difficult to accept. "We live our life as if we are never going to die and die as if we never lived," says the Dalai Lama.

The fear of death is at the heart of the human condition. We do not like to talk about it, especially not our own mortality. We all try to deny it. But when we live in denial of it, we unconsciously undervalue our present time. We might not care how much time has already passed, and we also waste it as if we're going to live forever.

If, on the other hand, we know our time will end one day, we will place a greater value on the things we do in the here and now. Every minute that we spend with a loved one, for instance, becomes infinitely more precious; every hour that is wasted becomes a great unrecoverable loss. Paradoxically, death is what gives life meaning, whereas that which makes life great is fleeting. Your ice cream tastes so good because it's about to melt. "Some things are more precious because they don't last long," says Oscar Wilde. And so are all the experiences worthy of spending your precious time on. They become more meaningful because they won't last too long.

An awareness of death gives life a sense of urgency; without it, life is taken for granted. **If you accept the unavoidability of death in a positive way, it will empower you to live your best life.** It will drive your ambition towards the legacy you want to leave behind.

If you can imagine your own obituary, what would you like people to say about you when you're gone? If you know the answer, start working towards that now. It will encourage you to take bold steps in choosing your life's purposes.

For a period of time Apple CEO and co-founder Steve Jobs knew he was dying and once said:

Remembering that I'll be dead soon is the most important tool I've ever encountered to help me make the big choices in life. Almost everything—all external expectations, all pride, all fear of embarrassment or failure—these things just fall away in the face of death, leaving only what is truly important. Remembering that you are going to die is the best way I know to avoid the trap of thinking you have something to lose. You are already naked. There is no reason not to follow your heart.

The Biggest Regret

A nurse who has counseled dying people in their last days has revealed what they regretted most was not being true to their dreams. The top regret expressed was essentially this: "I wish I'd had the courage to live a life true to myself, not the life others expected of me."

The biggest regret people have is when they realize their life is about to end, and they see how many of their dreams remain unfulfilled, mostly because of choices they made or did not make.

The second most common regret is, "I wish I hadn't worked so much."

Remember, there are seven days in a week—and "someday" isn't one of them. Choose the goals you are most passionate about and start working to achieve them. Life is short, and you should get the most out of it.

Understanding Your Success

Once you have determined the things that are important to you, you can start taking actions to achieve your goals. Remember: **things that divert you from those goals are essentially a waste of time, and things that bring you closer to living in alignment with your goals are the best**

use of your time.

Of course, easier said than done. Pursuing our dreams is not easy. We may know what we want, but it's not exactly clear how to get there. So sometimes we end up pursuing lesser goals that impede us from achieving our dreams. Or, when we hit an obstacle to our goal, it is easy to quit and settle for something less: "We are kept from our goal not by obstacles but by a clear path to a lesser goal," says Robert Brault, author of *Round Up the Usual Subjects*.

A lesser goal might offer a great short-term opportunity, but it's potentially a waste of time. That time could have been used to bring you closer to your true goal—and it's time you will never get it back. You are being driven by achievement. That's not the same as fulfillment, and it's not the same as success.

Fulfillment can only come from living in alignment with who you truly want to be and what you truly what to achieve.

As for success, we need to take a moment to examine what that is… because it sure as heck is not society's usual definition of success (succeeding at the goals or a job, or acquisition of material things).

YouTube star Casey Neistat defines success in the same way I do:

The ultimate quantification of success is not how much time you spend doing what you love. It's how little time you spend doing what you hate.

If your life is filled with things you hate to do, you will become stressed out by your internal conflict over this. You'll be aiming for short-term gains at the price of long-term losses. Instead, as you choose things to do during the day, ask yourself this question: will reaching this goal bring me closer to or further away from my major objectives in life?

Life is for living, and you are truly alive when you are living your dreams. Author Lewis Howes writes, "Your job is to create a vision that makes you want to jump out of bed in the morning. If it doesn't, go back to bed until you have a bigger dream."

The purpose of life is to enjoy it to the fullest. **By pursuing the things you are passionate about, you will live a life of purpose—and that's the true purpose of life.**

Time Miracle Task

List the top 3 'Flow' activities that put you "Into the Zone."

1. _____

2. _____

3. _____

How does each make you feel? Does it contribute to your overall life satisfaction?

1. _____

2. _____

3. _____

What can you do to improve on that?

_____

_____

_____

What would you do if you had only one year to live?

_____

_____

_____

PART 4

"STRETCHING" YOUR LIFE ESSENCE YEARS

14

Increase Your Life Savings

From "Zero-Days" to a Rich Life Story

∽◦∽

"If you want to live a memorable life, you have to be the kind of
person who remembers to remember."
– Joshua Foer

"In general, a time filled with varied and interesting experiences
seems short in passing but long as we look back. On the other
hand, a tract of time empty of experiences seems long in passing
but in retrospect short."
– William James

Time Flies as We Get Older

We all remember a time in our childhood when school years never
ended and summer vacations were ridiculously long; when the
weeks and months ran slow compared to how they now seem to fly. In
adulthood, weeks and months rush by at a seemingly accelerating pace,
and we look back and wonder, "Is it a new year already?"

Time seems to speed up as we grow older. That's a fact that we all
experience at some point in our life. The years seemingly get shorter and

shorter, and the remaining time that's available for us to live our lives diminishes with every round and cannot be regained.

As much as we would like, we can't add more time; it's a finite and constantly diminishing resource. But we *can* learn to subjectively "stretch" those life essence years and spend them in a more satisfying way.

To do that, we will need to **find ways to make time run slowly in our minds—back to the speed it used to run when we were children—so that we can make the most of it.** For that, we'll need to explore how our brains perceive time in a bit more detail , as well as other factors that speed up time in the first place.

Who Am I?

Neuroscientists have reached the conclusion that what makes up your "self"—that authentic voice in your head that you undoubtedly refer as "you"—is just an illusion! While you might feel you are an individual who has one single indivisible self, scientists have shown that our brains are composed of several decentralized modules with no central command center. Essentially, there is no Wizard running Oz.

One piece of intriguing evidence that supports this conclusion comes from split-brain patients: epileptic people whose thick neural cable that connects their brain's left and right hemispheres was cut to alleviate their seizures. The brain's left hemisphere specializes in speech and controls the right side of the body; the right controls the left side of the body. Researchers found that, when the cable connecting to the two hemispheres was severed, not only did each half have no idea what was going on in the other, but each half-brain had different plans in mind. One patient, for instance, reported that when his right hand would reach out to open a door, his left hand would intervene and try to shut it!

Also, when an image was shown to a patient's right eye, it registered in the left hemisphere controlling speech, and the patient could say what they saw. But when the image was shown to the left eye, it registered in the right hemisphere, which has no access to the vocal–language ability. It turns out the patient wouldn't be able to say what the image was, but they could spell it out with their left hand using Scrabble tiles.

Countless studies have shown that **there are at least two streams of consciousness inside our brain.** The brain's right side (our "experiencing self") experiences things exactly as they are happening around us but remembers nothing. The left side (our "remembering self") plays the role of internal storyteller that interprets those experiences.

Nobel Prize winner Daniel Kahneman describes these two brain systems extensively in his best-selling book, *Thinking Fast and Slow*. The "remembering self" is the slow, deliberate, analytical, and conscious system that makes sense of the world. The "experiencing self" is the fast, automatic, intuitive, and largely unconscious system. The "remembering self" interprets the behaviors, thoughts, and emotions being experienced. It goes over them to censor moments of horror, keep the pleasant parts, throw away the unimportant, add in a dash of fantasy… and then stores in our memory a story with a happy ending. **As a result, the stories created by our "remembering self" are fluffy and almost always inaccurate.** It's the part of our brain that's calling all the shots and hard choices of life: career, partner, where you live, where you take your holidays, etc. The "remembering self" is what creates the illusion that we've got a unified operation inside our head that's running the show. It creates our sense of self and free will—yet our "experiencing self" cannot be ignored.

Remembering Happy Times

Our brains measure happiness in two ways as well. What makes our "experiencing self" happy is not the same as what makes our "remembering self" happy. The "remembering self," for instance, does not care how long a pleasant or unpleasant experience lasts, but is only interested in the *peak* level of pleasure or pain, and by the way the experience *ends*. This is called the "peak–end rule," and it determines what memories end up being remembered.

One study, for instance, found that college students' decisions on whether or not they would repeat a spring-break vacation depended on the most pleasant moment of the previous vacation and how that vacation ended, not by how much fun the prior vacation was moment by moment.

The peak–end rule is why pediatricians keep in their clinics jars full of sweets to give to children after a painful vaccine injection. When the child's remembering self recalls the visit to the doctor, one minute of a pleasant treat at the end will wipe out fifteen minutes of pain. The same goes for women undergoing childbirth. The pain is so intense that it is surprising women are still willing to go through it again. However, evolution has wired women's hormonal system to secrete certain chemicals that create feelings of ecstasy when the baby is born. As a result, the end of the traumatic childbirth experience ends up being remembered positively.

The *remembered* happiness or pain from an event is more important than the happiness or pain experienced *during* that event—and that is also crucial for our experience of time.

The Time–Perception Paradox

In the same way, time is perceived differently by our "experiencing self" and "remembering self." The "experienced duration" of a social dinner is how your "experiencing self" feels time is passing while you are *at that dinner*—a period that is almost always different from the "remembered duration" that your "remembering self" recalls a few days later. This creates a subjective paradox in our time perception.

The reason for those discrepancies is because **"experienced durations" depend on how aware (or distracted) you are of the passing time, whereas "remembered durations" depend on the amount of memories you retain from the activity you were engaged in.**

For instance, when you are absorbed in a movie or reading a book, your inattention to the passing time will make that time pass quickly and the "experienced duration" will seem short. The opposite occurs when waiting in a long queue. Time drags and the "experienced duration" will seem long because your attention to the passing time is high.

In contrast, the "remembered duration" of a good night's sleep feels only a few seconds long because, during sleep, no new memories are captured. When you wake up, you get the impression that the whole night only lasted for a few moments, or as if time flew. Compare that to an exciting night out that is spent with friends. When later recalled, there are so many "memory markers" that it feels much longer than the night you spent sleeping

Moreover, **the "experienced duration" does not always match the "remembered duration" from the same event.** For instance, an interesting social dinner where you meet several new people and are absorbed in the conversations will pass very quickly, and you wonder how time flew. The dinner will be over "before you know it," and its "experienced duration" will be negligible because you paid no attention to the passing time. But when you recall that dinner a week later, its "remembered duration" will seem *long* because of all the interesting memories you retained from that event! Time flies when you're having fun, and so the "experienced durations" will feel short. But what's more important is that those memorable moments will create longer "remembered durations"—and this is what gets archived in your mind.

In contrast, time will drag at a boring dinner as you check your watch and wonder when it will be over. Your attention to the passing time will cause time to run slowly, and the "experienced duration" will seem long. But when you recall that dinner a week later, its "remembered duration" will be negligible because you can barely recall *any* memorable moments from that time. It soon will be forgotten as if it was never a part of your life.

Let's apply this understanding to something we all love to do: go on holiday.

If you take a vacation, for instance, to an entirely new place where you can experience exciting adventures and a new culture, taste new foods, listen to novel music, and observe new sights and sounds, there will be many opportunities to retain memorable moments—which will stretch that vacation's "remembered duration." But during that vacation time, you will be so absorbed with these novel experiences that your attention will be distracted from the passing time—i.e., "time flies when you are having fun." As soon as it is over, the vacation feels like it was "over in a flash"—and your "experienced duration" feels negligible. However, a few weeks later, when you recall that vacation, you realize that there was so much *novelty* to chew on, and so many memories to keep, that it makes your vacation seem longer than how it felt at the time. Those memorable moments somehow cause time intervals to "stretch" in your mind. Now your "remembered duration" will seem longer than the duration you experienced at the time.

If, on the other hand, you go on a vacation to a *familiar* beach resort, the opposite "time mismatch" occurs. While on holiday, you might spend the whole time in a relaxing mood, lying on the beach, reading a book, or enjoying the sun. Each and every day you repeat this same routine. Having escaped your work environment and all its distractions, you are now able to devote your full attention to that peaceful rest time, and as a result, the days drag and time slows down—so the "experienced duration" will seem long. However, once you are back at work and try to recall that vacation later on, it will seem short since you have collected only a few truly interesting memories from it. That experience might have been rejuvenating while you were living it, but the vacation will not register much time in your mind. Thus the "remembered duration" will feel shorter than what you experienced at the time.

Apply this understanding to when you catch the Flu and stay home from work for a few days. As you lie on the couch and flick through channels on the TV, you're horribly bored. You're lying around trying to conserve energy and get better, and there is not much to distract your attention from the passage of time. As a result, time feels like it's running very slowly when you are home sick. However, once you recover and look back at those days, it feels like they went by in a flash. That's because **nothing remarkable happened. No novelty, and thus very few "memory markers" retained in your mind.** The "experienced duration" of a few long boring days of illness equate to a negligible "remembered duration" in your memory—and, as time goes by, the whole period may be totally forgotten, as if it was never part of your life.

For a more detailed look on how our brains experience time and the various factors that affect our perceived speed of time, check out my previous book, *The Power of Time Perception*.

A Longer Life—through Memorable Moments

Now, back to the question of how to stretch those precious lifetime-essence years.

As we saw, **the number and intensity of our memories is what stretches our "remembered durations" and makes them *seem* long.** A "remembered duration" can span an interval of a few seconds to, in principle, a whole lifetime. Your memorable experiences affect how long you perceive last month, last year, the last decade, and even your whole life to be! Therefore, **the effect of memories on "remembered durations" does not only apply to daily activities** but can also be used to subjectively stretch those precious years of your life—and enhance your overall perception of leading a more fulfilling life!

When you recall an action-packed week, it feels longer than a typical-routine week, right? The same goes for months and years: the more memorable moments you can recall from them, the longer they seem. Without any significant memories, those months or years would simply fly. This key relationship between memories and the perceived duration of time intervals is very important to stretching our precious "life time essence."

When you look back at your life starting with your childhood, you get "flash-memories" of people, places, and events that happened long ago. They may be entirely banal—the smell of a leather armchair on a sunny day; the colorful pencil case you took to school; that vanilla smell coming from the ice cream van—but in their banality they infer the existence of your former self who lived those moments some remote time ago. The richer those memories, the longer your childhood will seem. On the other hand, if you barely remember anything from your childhood, it will seem as if it passed by quickly.

The same applies to all stages of your life. **The greater the variety of experiences you have and the more vivid your memories of them, the longer your life will seem.**

Zero-Days Add Up to Zero-Years!

Now, let's define a "zero-day" as being a day in which you didn't experience anything special that's worth remembering, did not create any memorable moments, or did nothing towards achieving your dreams.

Too many zero-days, and your life will fly by in a flash. Zero-days add up to zero-years, and not matter how many zeroes you add up, the sum will always be zero—in this case, a zero life.

In contrast, **"non-zero days" that create pleasant memories or contribute to your life's goals become part of your life story.** Your life story is like a lifetime-savings account that accumulates all the non-zero days in your life. **By spending your Life Essence years in non-zero days, you increase your "life savings"—and enrich your life story.**

A man who dies at the age of 40 might have subjectively lived longer than a man who dies at the age of 90, *if* he lived a life that's rich with the memorable moments of sensational experiences. Worse still for the 90-year-old would be reaching a point in his life when, for whatever reason, he goes on auto-pilot and simply stops living in the true sense of the word. It's as Benjamin Franklin once said: "Some people die at 25 and aren't buried until 75."

The difference between the two men is *their outlook on life*. One takes the initiative to make every day memorable with a mentality that is all about living life to the fullest. The other simply lets the events of his life control him and is swayed along with whatever the day brings—he lives a routine life full of zero-days.

A Great Life, or A Mediocre One?

The difference between a great life and a mediocre life is **the number of memorable moments that are collected over the course of lifetime.** A long and meaningful life does not depend on how much money or possessions you have, but rather on the unforgettable moments you collect along the way. Taking this logic to the extreme, living one moment in time that's worth a lifetime is far better than living one lifetime that's only worth a moment in time!

This has a major implication on how to stretch the lifetime-essence years that are available to enjoy life: **the more novelty you can introduce into your lifetime-essence years, the more memories you'll be able to create—and the longer those years will seem when you recall them.**

On the other hand, if you live a life of monotony, going through the same dull routine every day (driving the same darn route for your commute every day, for example), then your brain will not capture any interesting memories. Without any memory markers retained in your mind, time will fly, and days will slip into months, and then into years. Before you know it, you are about to celebrate your fortieth birthday and *The Simpsons* is already on Season 27!

Without memorable moments, life will be similar to one long good night's sleep that feels like only a few seconds long.

Don't get caught sleepwalking through 40 years of your life. **Life is not truly about the number of days you live, but the number of days you remember.** It is not measured by the number of breaths you take, but by the moments that take your breath away. Let's get the most out of life by creating some memorable moments and non-zero days to remember.

Where Do You Lie on the Scale of Life Fulfillment?

To find out where your life falls on the fulfillment scale, complete the next Time Miracle Task and find out how many non-zero days you have deposited from last month into your "lifetime savings account?"

Time Miracle Task

Write down as many non-zero days you remember from last month.

1. _____

2. _____

3. _____

4. _____

5. _____

6. _____

7. _____

8. _____

9. _____

10. _____

Divide the number of non-zero days by 30 and multiply by 100 to obtain the percentage of time you can recall on average.

If your score is less than 20 percent, then your life is mostly routine and you are not exposing yourself to many novel experiences. In the long run, this lack of variation and diversity will eventually lead to a less memorable life.

If your score is between 20 and 50 percent, than you're within the average.

Anything more than 50 percent is great! You are enjoying more novel experiences and recalling more non-zero days and, in the long run, you will enjoy a more fulfilling life.

15

Seek Novelty

∽

"Habit and routine have an unbelievable power to
waste and destroy."
– Henri de Lubac

What Kind of Person Are You?

When it comes to creating memorable experiences to stretch your time experience, **novelty** is a key ingredient. *Your brain is built to ignore the familiar and focus on the new.* When you pay attention to what is going on around you, your brain will pick out novelty before anything else. A new phone, visiting a new place, a new working environment, a new hair color, a new friend—they catch your eye, don't they? Anything unexpected— whether a small detail or a big event—that makes an appearance in our life is memorable. This makes sense from an evolutionary survival standpoint, since there is no point in wasting time to notice things that don't change from day to day.

The urge to seek novel experiences varies from one person to another; some of us are simply born with a brain that craves anything new… while others want to avoid change and novelty as much as possible.

In psychology, novelty-seeking is a personality "temperament" that is associated with the desire to explore new things. What temperament do you have?

If you are high on novelty-seeking, you are a "neophiliac." You...

- get bored easily
- are spontaneous, and won't be constrained by rules and regulation
- tend to be impulsive when it comes to making your decisions
- don't care much about spending money if it gets you the reward you crave

If, on the other hand, you are low on novelty-seeking, you are "neophobic." You...

- prefer to stick to "tried and tested"
- reflect on the pros and cons before making a decision
- tend to be reserved about spending money
- are more disciplined
- don't mind sticking to a routine

Each personality type has its benefits and drawbacks. In our case, seeking out new situations is great since that leads to memorable moments that will stretch your perceived Life Essence. It will also make you more curious and creative. Some studies even show that high novelty-seekers are happier and healthier.

But being a neophiliac also means you are more likely to be impulsive. That might not be as desirable, because it can lead to rash choices that you might later regret. You might also be extravagant, which leads to spending sprees that put you in financial difficulties.

Meanwhile, there are actually some benefits to being a neophobic and creating repetitive habits. By automating routine behavior, you can do things without thinking. It conserves brain power and enhances productivity.

But you won't enjoy much of life if every minute of your day is filled with routine. When you reflect back on your life, your constant abiding by routines will make the time fly. A neophobic will perceive his life to have passed faster, and therefore find it is shorter, than a neophiliac of the same age. Too much routine can also lead to boredom, which is unhealthy.

There are studies that show people living a dull lifestyle are 40 percent more likely to die early. They are literally bored to death!

Seek and Your Brain Shall Reward

But what makes you a neophiliac, a neophobic—or someone in-between? It all depends on a small part of your brain that evolved to create a desire for stimulation. It's a biochemical system that rewards you with pleasant sensations when you seek actions that increase your chances of survival and reproduction.

The brain juice that runs this "seeking system" is dopamine. The brain's dopamine circuitry is what stimulates your craving, and makes you feel good about it. Your brain is wired in such a way that causes you to constantly search for food, to survive, and mate to reproduce.

This is why the nice taste of food and the blissful orgasms don't last that long: if you want to feel them again you need to look for more food and have more sex. If you are able to somehow devise a way to enjoy everlasting sensations of bliss after eating or having sex, you would certainly live an extremely happy life—but it would be an awfully short one as well. That's because you wouldn't be bothered to look for more food and sex, and that would be the end of your descendants. That's why we are never fully satisfied and are constantly pursuing new ways to make us happy. Whatever you think might make you happy now—like winning the lottery or buying a Ferrari—can only last for a limited time before you get used to it and start seeking something new. **Our brains are built to reward the act of seeking—not the end result.**

In 1954, psychologist James Olds and his team were studying how rats learned[26]. They stuck electrodes in rats' brains and gave them small electric shocks every time they approached one particular corner of their cage. After a few shocks, the rats learned to avoid that corner. One day, while they were repeating the experiment, they inserted the probe in the wrong place by mistake. Instead of avoiding the corner where shocks were received, the rats kept returning to it over and over again. The rats were then given a lever that they could press to activate their own shocks… and they kept pressing it until they collapsed.

Olds assumed he must have discovered the brain's pleasure center, but what he actually found was the brain's seeking system. That area of the brain is what creates feelings of curiosity, interest, and anticipation. It's shared by all mammals and drives them to search and seek new things. With animals in a zoo, it causes them to prefer searching for their food than having it delivered to them.

In humans, it's what gets us out of bed each day to venture out into the world. It's why climbing mount Everest is more exciting than standing at the top; why flirting and foreplay are more exciting than an orgasm; and why kids prefer to play video games than come down for dinner. Like the rats pressing the pedal over and over again, it's the thrill that comes from killing a monster on a computer screen or watching the stock market rise and fall that hooks up people and creates the need for a new kick every day. It's what hooks you to your emails, Facebook feeds,

Twitter, and other social media—the excitement that accompanies your drive to search for novelty in so many other areas of your life.

Incredible excitement accompanies our drive to search for novelty in so many other areas of our life as well.

The novelty-seeking trait is an inherited trait, and we all have a certain amount of it. It is also linked to risk-taking, impulsiveness, and adventure-seeking. Risk-taking and novelty-seeking are also the hallmark of successful entrepreneurs and business persons. Yet they are also behind the rise in materialism, and the obsession with possessing new gadgets and material goods.

Satisfying "the Urge"

The urge for novelty-seeking that's genetically built into your personality defines the amount of novel experiences you need to consume over time. *You* define what that novelty means to you, and how much you need it depending on that innate personality trait.

If you are neophobic, you might be happy experiencing something new once a week or maybe even once a month. Novelty might simply mean trying a different dish from the one you usually pick from the menu.

Conversely, if you are a neophiliac, you might need something new every day. It might mean taking a vacation to a country that you've never visited before where you don't know anyone. Your brain's unique novelty-seeking level determines how easily you get bored, setting up a demand for stimulation that needs to be met.

It is a kind of supply-and-demand equation. On one side, your personality trait demands a certain amount of novelty that is genetically defined by your brain's dopamine system. On the other side of the equation, you live a lifestyle that supplies a certain amount of novelty into your life. You are happier when your lifestyle supplies enough novelty to match that innate demand—and less happy when it falls short.

At the Root of Our Unhappiness

Historically speaking, the supply of novelty has been declining with changes in our lifestyle. Through the last 200,000 years of our evolution, we lived a life that was short and brutal, but highly non-repetitive. For 99 percent of our history we were hunters and gatherers; as such, our brains became trained for survival in a challenging world that was constantly changing. Our ancestors were exposed to a high level of daily novelty (lions, tigers, and bears... oh, my), with action-packed days full of new surprises.

In the last one percent of our history, things started to change. With the advent of the Agricultural Revolution, man invented efficient ways to get more food for less work. Yet this also created a repetitive, routine life that contained less novel experiences.

The Industrial Revolution again changed the type of work we had to do to survive. It increased material wealth through mass production and extended life expectancy, but it also made daily life more dull and monotonous. Doing the same thing over and over wasn't inspiring or healthy. As routine increased, the opportunities for creating interesting memories decreased, and the feeling that time was moving faster grew stronger.

Our digital revolution has made things worse: working alone in a windowless cubicle or at a desk within a large open space day-after-day is not what our brains have evolved to do. Little differentiates one day from another, and with no new work memories worth retaining, the days and months fly at an accelerating pace.

Emotions, eating habits, desires, and sexuality that evolved 200,000 years ago based on a hunter-gatherer brain are now immersed in a post-industrial environment of mega-cities, trains, cars, computers, and cell phones. As author Yuval Noah Harari puts it in *Homo Deus*, "Today we may be living in high-rise apartments with over-stuffed refrigerators, but our DNA still thinks we are in the savannah."

The routine life we currently live has less and less novel experiences—one of the main reasons why we feel time is running faster. It is also at the root of our unhappiness.

Novelty Across a Lifetime

Our supply of novel experiences always declines as we age.

When you were young, novelty came naturally: everything was new. There were so many experiences to discover, interesting things to observe, and a whole world to explore. This constant supply of novelty matched your innate demand level, and childhood is generally a happy affair. During that stage, you absorb so many fascinating memories that when you recall them later, it seems like that childhood period stretched forever, and as if time ran slowly. That's why school years and summers never seemed to end when you were a kid.

The amount of novelty continues to increase as you grow into a teen. Between the ages of fifteen and twenty-five, there are new experiences to explore and more freedom. There are more "firsts," and these memories are usually densely packed. There is a first love, first kiss, first alcoholic drink, first sexual relationship, and first time away from home. Psychologists refer to that period as the "reminiscent bump." You can easily recall these rich memories because they occurred during formative years when your identity was being consolidated. These novel experiences created so many memory markers that when you recall them, the "remembered duration" will appear to have taken longer than it actually did. Time will again seem to have been running slowly. Supply of novelty generally meets demand.

But when you hit your thirties, you start to settle in, and your lifestyle starts to become more organized and predictable. You may find a steady job and establish a family with the usual kind of home chores and rhythm that repeats itself week after week. The amount of new experiences decreases, and things become much more familiar. The supply of novelty drops as you slowly lose that childish sense of wonder. You gradually stop paying conscious attention to the things around you: the town you live in, the buildings, streets, and your route to work. Your brain starts ignoring those and ceases to notice the small details that makes one day different from another. With fewer unique memories being captured, that period of time will seem shorter. Time starts to fly. That's why childhood years that are full of rich memories will seem longer than adulthood years.

When you feel that the years are "flying by," routine and monotony are the culprits.

Living on Autopilot

A varied, diverse, and fulfilled life is also a long one. By combatting the decline in novelty that naturally occurs in adulthood, we should be able to make those years seem longer. When we inject more novelty into our lives from our mid-life and onwards, it will cause time to subjectively slow down back to the speed it was running when we were children.

While engaging in novel experiences and creating memories might distract your attention from the "experienced time" that is passing—time flies when you are having fun—what is more important is that it will **create a dense mosaic of long-term memories which, when later**

recalled, will stretch the "remembered time" and enrich the story of your life.

Failing to do so will cause decades to pass in the blink of an eye and have dire consequences to your overall well-being. While some routine in life is good, too much is bad for you.

Most people are letting time pass by. They are "passing through," letting every day be just like the day before, and the day before. Letting things happen and letting time tick away—fast.

When you live a routine life, you do the same mundane things, in the same order, day after day after day. This lifestyle puts your brain on autopilot, and as a result, no memory markers are captured and time passes by quickly. Spending your weekdays waiting for the weekend and months waiting for your next vacation becomes a total waste. Zero-days that are devoid of anything new will pass by unnoticed and be forgotten, as if they were never part of your life. So much of your life will be missed in those "autopilot times" because you'd be living it without ever truly experiencing the moments in a memorable way.

Psychological stress also starts building up as the supply of novelty falls below the demand that's built into your personality and genes. Then, one day, you wake up and realize that more than half of your life is over and you do not really have much to show for it. You feel like life has passed you by, and you missed the chance to really enjoy it as much as you would have liked to. You start asking yourself, "What happened to all those great times I was meant to have and all those dreams I planned to achieve? Is this really it?"

On top of all that, you start having body aches, wrinkles, and poor eyesight. You realize that every year is feeling shorter and your time is drawing near. Existential questions start popping up in your mind like,

"What am I living for," or, "What's the meaning of my life?" or, "Is my job truly what I'm meant to do?" "Is my partner truly the person I should be with?" or, "Is this city truly where I should be living?" You look at some of the opportunities you missed or the bad decisions you made and you wonder how things might have been… Would you have experienced more memorable moments and be happier, had you taken that job, or married that girl, or moved into that other city?

Midlife crisis kicks in the moment you realize you have been living on autopilot for your entire life. Time is running out, and you haven't enjoyed life like you really wanted to.

Each one of us will react differently to this awareness of the impending end that is creeping up on us. Some will try to confront it by tackling the age-related symptoms. They might go on a diet, join a gym, or endure plastic surgery. Or they might buy a motorbike or a sports car… anything to make them feel young again.

Others will lose themselves to alcohol, drugs, sex, or exotic pleasures—anything that keeps their mind free of the nagging question, "Is this really it?"

Some will find answers in religion or alternative spiritualties. Other will start volunteering, supporting charitable causes, or finding new purpose for their *raison d'etre*.

In many cases, it will be time to discard old beliefs and create an entirely new way of life that's more in sync with what makes you happy. Whatever it is, you're the captain of your own ship—*and only you can figure it out.*

Captain Your Ship

It's never too late to be whomever you want to be, experience things that you've never felt before, and live a life of which you're proud.

No one said it better than the Welsh poet Dylan Thomas: "Do not go gently into that good night. Rage, rage against the dying of the light."

Or, if you haven't reached that phase of life yet, please realize it is important to combat the decline in novelty early on and avoid reaching a mid-life crisis.

In the next few chapters, we will look at ways for collecting memories and introducing as much novelty for the purpose of living a memorable life. Remember that life is not the number of days you live, but the number of days you remember.

You don't have to test your DNA to find out how much novelty-seeking is in your personality. The following short quiz will help.

Time Miracle Task

Complete the Novelty-Seeking Personality Quiz by clicking the link below or answering the following questions

https://goo.gl/forms/3TafOCxgLrtlXegn1

Answer the following questions to calculate the level of novelty-seeking in your personality

1. If you had all the money you need, where would you spend your next vacation?
   a. On the beach
   b. In Antarctica
   c. Diving the deepest oceans

2. Would you go into outer space if you had the chance?
   a. No way
   b. Perhaps
   c. In a heartbeat!

3. If you had magical powers, what method of transportation would you prefer?
   a. I am fine with a car, thanks
   b. Flying goose
   c. Can I Teleport?

4. Which is most important to you?

    a. Safety

    b. Novelty

    c. Excitement

5. How many countries have you travelled to?

    a. Less than 2

    b. Between 3 and 6

    c. More than 7

6. Do you talk to strangers?

    a. No

    b. Sometimes

    c. Yes

7. Your friends would probably describe you as

    a. Not really adventurous

    b. Kind of adventurous

    c. Adventurous

Time to calculate your Novelty-Seeking score.

- For every (a) answer, give yourself 1 point.
- For every (b) answer, give yourself 2 points.
- For every (c) answer, give yourself 3 points.

Add up the points from each of the questions above and calculate the total score.

Time Miracle Task

What Is Your Novelty-Seeking Score? _____

1. If your novelty-seeking score is between 7 and 11, you are mostly neophobic.
2. If your novelty-seeking score is between 12 and 16, you have an average novelty-seeking personality.
3. If your novelty-seeking score is between 17 and 21, you are a neophiliac.

16

Reclaim Lost Childhood Memories

Mental Time Travel

∞

"Sometimes you will never know the value of a moment until it
becomes a memory."

– Dr. Seuss

The Snapshots of Our Life

When we think back on our life, our past is made up of a series of
mental snapshots starting from our earliest memories, all the way
through the various defining moments in our life: the good, the bad, the
happy, the sad, the mistakes we made, and the lessons we learned. We
view our lifespan in terms of the number of unique memories we have
acquired—which comprise the number of non-zero days we retain in our
mind.

Memories are invaluable things in life that can't be replaced. They
are like those things that you can't buy, but that matter the most like
health, happiness, and love. Your graduation day, the day you got married,
having your first child, etc. It is, therefore, important to spend your Life

Essence years collecting and retaining as many memorable moments as possible, so that when you recall your past, you'll be satisfied that you have lived a long and fulfilling life.

Recalling a positive past is essential to your happiness and sense of well-being. **The richer in memories and novel experiences your life is, the longer and more fulfilling it will be.**

So, how do you collect more memories and move up on the scale of life fulfillment? Where do we start? With your childhood.

Fish Them Out

If you struggle to remember your early childhood years, you're not alone. As we grow older, those early years fade away and are forgotten, as if they were never part of our life. They are distilled into just a few moments' worth of memories that, according to psychologists, form the foundation upon which a personality is built. That time is an important part of our life story, and the way we remember it determines the kind of person we turn out to be.

Many of us would like to recall the things we did, the friends we made, the streets, houses, and playgrounds we grew up in, right? If we could go back in time and relive our childhood one more time, we would try to save those memories to savor them later. But traveling physically back in time is, of course, not possible. *Mental* time travel, on the other hand, is feasible and the best way to re-awaken those ephemeral childhood memories that lie dormant deep inside your mind.

Still, having a perfect memory capable of recalling the smallest details of our lives is not possible; evolution doesn't allow us such unlimited memory capacity because it is not critical to our survival. In fact, our brains cannot remain efficient if we do *not* forget. The side effect from this auto-erasing mechanism is that it takes away crucial ingredients from our life story. So, is there a way to recover some of that forgotten childhood?

Write 'em Up

Neurologist Richard Restak suggest that you can reacquaint yourself with your emotions by writing a letter to your younger self.

Start by finding an object from your childhood—perhaps a stuffed animal or toy—that takes you back in time down your memory lane. It could be a photo of yourself when you were young. Focus on it for a while, including where it was taken and what were you doing. Then, imagine yourself as your young self, and write a letter to your older self about the dreams you had, the things you wanted to achieve, and your hopes and worries about the future. Write to your heart's content, using crayons if you desire. Follow that up with a letter from the older, current you to your younger self describing your future, the things you will end up doing, and who you will grow up to be.

By doing this simple exercise, you might discover feelings that you have not experienced in years or expose memories that were long forgotten.

Another few tips to help you out:

- **Meet up with an old childhood friend.** Talk about what you did together. The reunion will stir up many memories that will help you recollect many forgotten aspects of your life.
- **Return to the house and place you grew up in.** This will refresh your mind about many things you used to do as a child.
- **Create a Family Memory Book.** Start with how you met your partner, how you got married, and have each member of your family contribute with their favorite memories.

- **Have a Weekly "Memory Discussion" Family Dinner.** Dedicate some time to sit with your family and recall things you did together. You can do that with your friends as well. Their memories help to bring up yours.

Whatever you fish out from the depth of your mind will enrich your life story and add to your lifetime-essence savings account so that your life will seem longer and more fulfilling.

Your Life Story

Memories are your life. They are solely yours and yours alone. The things you did, the laughs you laughed, the tears you shed—they make up your life. But they can be easy to forget, so let's not.

When you recall memories, some will make you smile, some will make you wiser, and others will make you cry. All, however, are crucial for generating a memorable life and a rich life story.

Without memories, you would find yourself asking, "Where did all those years go?" The days would slip out of your hands and into the depth of the forgotten past.

But if you can look back at your life and say that you made the most of every moment, then you are richer than you know, not necessarily with wealth and money, but life-rich—and you'll stop asking, "How did the time fly on by?"

You will remember exactly how.

Time Miracle Task

Dig out an object from your childhood or a photo of yourself when you were young. Focus on it and imagine you are your young self. List all the dreams you wanted to achieve. Write down any worries you had.

1. _____
2. _____
3. _____
4. _____
5. _____

Now imagine you are writing a letter to your younger self about your future. List the things you will end up doing and who you will grow up to be.

1. _____
2. _____
3. _____
4. _____
5. _____

After completing this, reflect on those long-forgotten feelings and memories you just discovered.

17

Energize Your Leisure Time

A Step Outside the Ordinary

∽

"The one thing that you have that nobody else has is you. Your
voice, your mind, your story, your vision. So, write and draw
and build and play and dance and live as only you can."
— **Neil Gaiman**

Energize Leisure Activities

We all wish to spend our Life Essence years in some form of
leisure, right? But having leisure time in abundance does not
automatically mean we are making memorable moments during that
time. There are multi-millionaires who do not work and have all the free
time in the world, yet chances are that many spend it doing nothing
worthwhile.

When our leisure time is devoid of goals and challenges, it becomes
meaningless, often leading us to depression and addictions. Therefore, to
enhance our quality of life and our perceived lifetime longevity, we need
to learn how to use our Life Essence to **achieve goals that contribute to
our life satisfaction and doing the things we enjoy.**

The types of memories you ultimately can forge from novel leisure-time activities will differ depending on the kind of leisure in which you engage:

- **"Active leisure"** constitutes those times in which you experience *high motivation.* For example, you might become engrossed in playing sports, exercising, creating art, making music, or engaging in interesting dialogue.

- **"Passive leisure"** refers to those times in which you experience *low motivation.* This is when you might be engaged in media consumption, like watching TV and listening to music, or lying on the beach.

The novelty that arises from active leisure pursuits creates a more intense experience than the novelty that arises from passive leisure pursuits.

To best understand this, spend an entire day on the couch watching TV. That's right. I am actually advising you to **watch TV** here! Specifically, try to view on that day an entire season of a TV series you have not seen before, to ensure the show contains a lot of novelty.

Next, spend one day exploring a new city on foot or on bike, during which you are just physically moving through space without stopping (except for a breather and a bite or two).

Which day feels longer in retrospect? A week later, when you recall that day, which one was fuller and richer? Even though both types of leisure introduced novelty in some form to us, it was *active* physical movement *that injected intensity into the novel experiences—and caused time to slow down in retrospect.*

This is not to say that passive leisure is a poor use of time. Enjoying some peaceful relaxation can be exceedingly rewarding. But research confirms that **being immersed in a highly motivating challenge is more likely to make us happy, and we will perceive it later as time that was well spent.**

Making Memory Anchors

High-motivation leisure makes it is easier to enter into a state of flow or being "in the zone." Also, flow-inducing activities create richer memories or "memory markers" when compared to passive fun activities. You might enjoy watching TV for a couple of hours, but a few days later, when you try to recall that time, there may be no trace of it in your memory. **Without enough memory anchors, time will fly.** Spending most of your free time on passive activities therefore won't add much to your life fulfillment. Conversely, a couple of hours spent on a hiking trip could produce many more memories that will last for years in your mind. They'll enrich your past, causing it to appear longer than it really is.

Of course, you have to be realistic in how memorable you can make your time. It is easy to make memories when you are on vacation or during special events, but it's not realistic for every day to be some novel grand experience! There simply are days when you have to take the trash out, get on a bus, or stand in the checkout line of a grocery store—and none of these events are particularly memorable. **But it's the contrast between the ordinary and the exciting that makes something remarkable.** Without any "checkout line moments," the excitement of what you consider memorable becomes unnoticeable.

The key is trying to find a balance and create a sufficiently exciting lifestyle so you won't get lost in forgotten zero-days. This can be done by seeking tiny bits of novelty in all things so that you are constantly capturing memories on a daily basis. Break free from the "autopilot life mode"—**and embrace novelty in the routine of your daily life**.

Every day has the potential to be memorable, and your life will seem longer if you make a little effort to make it so.

One Step Outside Routine

You can experience perceived lifetime longevity if you have the ability to collect pleasant memories from BOTH the ordinary AND the extraordinary. One way to handily do this is to step outside your normal routines—even through taking just one small step—to incorporate novel experiences that stimulate you in some way.

You do *not* have to participate in extreme sports such as skydiving, rock climbing, or surfing to create excitement and novelty. You don't need to compete in the Olympics. Thankfully, it doesn't truly matter what the new experience is. **What matters is how it makes you** *feel*.

Here's how you can easily experience novelty on a daily basis, and stretch out your time in your life…

- **Spend some time with nature—even if you just happen to be in your own yard.** Look up in the trees on your property; is there a bird's nest you never noticed? Did you ever try to climb up a few branches on a tree perfect for climbing? Is there a frog caught in a window well that could need a rescue? Hey, wait… is that a rainbow over there?

- **While on your commute to work, stop somewhere new for a coffee, drive a different route, or choose a different kind of transport** (a bus instead of the train, for example). You do not have to travel far to experience novelty.

- **Get to know cultures that are different than yours** by trying different ethnic restaurants, cooking exotic dishes, or gaining exposure to a new foreign language.

- **Go listen to live music—music of all kinds,** whether jazz, classical, rap, or the blues. You might be able to find many tickets that are lower-priced or for free if local religious institutions or churches offer music programs (many do).

- **Play about… by taking in a play.** Same advice here as when it comes to music. Sure you can spend a fortune going to see a show on Broadway and it'll be great, but you can also have a great time being in the audience at a community theatre or a school play.

- **Change the way you wear your hair today!**

- **Get out of a clothing rut and put on different attire than what's typical for you.** Wear a scarf if you never do so; if you're a jeans gal, don a dress. If you never wear skinny jeans paired with a long sweater, try the combination. If you're a guy who dresses down, throw on a jacket and tie one day. Even deciding to wear a pair of funky socks to work can make a difference. *Change doesn't have to be big.*

- **Experience novelty in your neighborhood.** Take a salsa dance class, walk your dog down some unfamiliar streets over the weekend, or try a new item on a restaurant menu. Look around the corner; is there perhaps a new restaurant, gift shop, or coffee shop that you have never tried? *Rather than sticking to the usual familiar places, try something new.*

- **If you are an avid reader of e-books, take a page out of the book of another generation, and visit the local library.** Browse the shelves; are there topics that you've never considered reading about before that look intriguing? Check out books on those topics. If you're looking for a good fiction read, select works by authors you've never tried before. If you read all the time, select an audiobook or a podcast for a change in routine.

- **Go out for a dinner with your family or, if you've been dining outside a lot, cook dinner at home instead.**
- **Play games, chat with your spouse or kids, and spend time in cultural pursuits.**

Whatever feels great will last a lifetime.

Streeetccchhh Out the Time

New sounds, people, tastes, colors, textures, and smells send massive information to your brain and provide lasting memories which, when recalled, will cause your time to stretch. These higher-value memories you've created will stick around in your mind for a long time. Plus, the more higher-value memories you accumulate, the larger your lifetime savings.

We already saw how addiction to social media can become a major waste of our precious time. But a few social media channels have a few useful features. One way, for instance, of keeping those memorable moments alive and fresh is to store them on Facebook or Instagram. Through social media, you can keep all such memories on a timeline and create snapshots from the important events of your life that can be quickly recalled anytime and anywhere. You no longer have to rely on your imperfect brain to preserve those precious memories.

Remember that excessive time spent on social media consumption is a waste. That time is better spent in enhancing life fulfillment. But not all social media is useless. With Facebook, for instance, you are able to pick a date at random and look at the photos of what happened on that date or in that year, the friends you were interacting with, and the "status updates" you were posting. So, you can relive the day your child was born, that incredible Christmas gathering, the rockin' New Year party, your romantic vacation to Paris—and even those mundane everyday memories where there was a slight twist. All of this will help you maintain fresh memories of valuable moments in time that otherwise would have been forgotten.

The richness of these memories will, when combined over long periods of time, stretch the months and years that make up your perceived life span and contribute to your overall life satisfaction.

Build Anticipation

Anticipation of a positive event slows down time, so introducing anticipation into your life helps in slowing it down.

When you have to wait for something nice to happen, time feels like it runs more slowly. The week leading to Christmas day always seems to drag. So does the work week leading to a vacation.

Anticipation also increases the intensity of our emotions—and intense emotions slow the speed of time. Most people experience deep emotional reactions, for instance, when they are anticipating their Thanksgiving holiday, much more so than then when they later recall it.[27] Anticipation is much more intense than retrospection, because future events are less certain than past events, and uncertainty amplifies emotions. When you are emotional, you feel time is running slower.

In most cases, positive anticipation might be annoying, so why not use this to your advantage? For instance, deliberately build anticipation and excitement when planning a date or organizing a long summer vacation. That anticipation will increase your alertness level and direct your attention to the passing time, causing it to "slow down" in a pleasant and exciting way.

Research on how people enjoy their vacations[28] has shown that anticipating and planning a vacation can end up being even more enjoyable than the vacation itself! That's because people look forward to their vacations and, for most, the enjoyment starts weeks, even months, before the vacation actually starts.

Researchers from the Netherlands surveyed 1,530 Dutch vacationers and measured their happiness levels before and after they took their vacation.[28] **The largest boost in happiness that was reported came from the simple act of *planning* the vacation.** In other words, expecting a good thing is sometimes more enjoyable than actually experiencing it.[29]

It stands to reason therefore that you can get more fun out of several small vacations in a year than from one big one. Two one-week long holidays are probably better than one two-week holiday, which is probably better than a one-month long holiday. Of course, longer holidays are great in terms of allowing us to switch off from responsibilities and work. But more vacations, however short their actual duration, create more excitement and more things to look forward to during the year. They also create more memory markers during the year that makes that year seem richer and more fulfilling.

Moments of eager anticipation heighten our mental arousal—and slow down time. *The more anticipation you can create, the slower time will seem to flow.*

You can apply this principle to any area of your life. Every day, make sure you always have something to anticipate, something nice to wake up to in the morning, or an exciting thing to do after work.

Each of these could be something simple and quite doable, and therefore easy to work into a daily routine. Anticipate seeing a close friend you haven't seen in a while; visualize a hobby like playing the drums or going biking on the weekend; or plan on having a great dinner one weeknight.

Anything that excites you and spurs your creative juices will make you happier. Moreover, having constant anticipation in your life will slow time down, and make your life seem longer.

Socialize and Laugh More

Relationships are not just important for your overall happiness, but they generate memorable moments that enrich life. Family and friendships are great conductors of happiness. And meeting new people provides your brain with a lot of information to chew on, such as their characters, accents, voices, facial expressions, and body language. It also gives you the opportunity to share ideas, see problems from a new perspective, and receive insight in ways you never thought of before.

According to the American Time Use Survey of 2016, the average American spends about 39 minutes each day socializing, such as visiting friends or attending or hosting social events. This was the next most common leisure activity after watching TV. Over the course of one lifetime, this adds up to 1.6 years spent socializing. Out of that, people spend, on average, six minutes laughing each day—or around four months over a lifetime.

Unfortunately, it seems that in these busy modern times, the time we spend laughing has been declining. A similar survey done back in the 1950s showed we used to laugh three times as long. Let's change that by stepping away from the media and stepping up to those who we love, those whom we don't know, and those who intrigue us! Here's some simple ways to start engaging in more social interactions on a daily basis:

A great way to socialize is to join a social club, book club, sports club, or a hobby group where you can constantly meet new people. The resulting meaningful and interesting social interactions will create long-term memories that will stretch your Life Essence years.

Spice Up Your Life

Each and every day, cultivate your relationships. Spice up your days through adding a little novelty to what's ordinary. Anticipate the fun times that are coming in your life and engage in active leisure pursuits; all are great ways for creating memory markers and your unforgettable life story.

A life full of memorable moments and novel experiences is a long, rich, and fulfilling life. Without memories you will find yourself asking "where did all those years go?" Without memories the days would slip out of your hands and into the depths of the forgotten past. But if you make the most of every moment, you will be richer than you know, not necessarily with wealth and money, but life-rich.

Time Miracle Task

Based on this chapter's numerous suggestions, make at least three commitments for next month that will help you stretch your time.

1. _____

2._____

3._____

18

Rich in Experience

Your Bucket List

ﾠ⌘ﾠ

"It's not the years in your life that count. It's the life in your years."
– Abraham Lincoln

And the Oscar Goes to…

It's time to decide how you want to spend your limited Life Essence. What difference do you want to make? It's time to fill your infinitely precious time with vibrant and intriguing experiences. It's time to reinvent yourself and live your life to the fullest.

Today is the first day of the rest of your life. It is special, because you're only going to live it once in a lifetime. So go ahead… create memorable moments. Promise yourself that there will be no more zero-days. Whatever you normally do every day, try something different today.

"It is how we choose what we do, and how we approach it, that will determine whether the sum of our days adds up to a formless blur, or to something resembling a work of art," wrote Mihaly Csikszentmihalyi.

Produce a rich life story worthy of an Oscar award. That's the secret of making your life memorable.

Don't Wait, Be Happy

I'm not going to be the one who says that saving money for retirement isn't a wise thing to do. But life has shown us that life is short and that we should eat, drink, and be merry while we still can.

Recent research by economists has confirmed that it is better to spend your money and be happy while you are young than save it for future spending in your older "golden" years. If you are constantly working for the future, planning for some endpoint when you'll reward yourself with the money you've saved and be happy, you'll end up missing the present for a future that may never come. Saving for your retirement is certainly wise, but this has to be balanced so that you are not always waiting to be happy but rather spending enough on experiences now to make life worth living.

Accumulating money isn't some vague goal towards which you should work; you should use money as a tool for living a decent life that generates memorable moments for a subjectively long and fulfilling life. Happiness comes when we spend our time and money on creating memorable moments through great experiences.

When you go to a travel agent or restaurant, you are not buying a plane ticket, hotel, or fancy dinner; you are buying an experience to remember. Remember, **novel experiences are the ingredients for memorable moments.** They convert typical zero-days to non-zero days.

Memorable non-zero days stretch your life, while zero-days only cause life to slip by.

Rich in Experience

In this age of seductive advertising, it is easy to get obsessed with consumerism and spending our money on material goods. So many of us work so hard to pay our bills and sustain a lifestyle that's driven by instant gratification. For many people, the pursuit of happiness boils down to buying the latest technology gadgets or clothes from this season's latest fashion trend. Sure, you may enjoy that new bag for a couple of months, but before you know it, you'll be planning the next purchase (most likely something you don't really need). The time you'll spend shopping (around two years of your life, if you shop for 6 hours each week) can also be reduced and put to better use.

Recent research[30] conducted by San Francisco State University has shown that **people are far happier when they spend money on experiences rather than material goods.** When you buy a new phone or car, your return on investment is the usage you will get out of it. But when you spend money on an experience, the memories generated are almost immeasurable. The boost in happiness you get when you buy a new phone or car eventually wears off, while experiences improve over time and can be relived for many years. Think about this: isn't it more likely that you remember your first hiking trip over your first pair of hiking boots?

Experiences are also *unique*—whereas material things are not. When you compare your possessions with others, you might become unhappy because there is always someone who has the "better" car or house. *But no one else's experiences can compare with the experiences* you *had!*

No one will ever have the same experience you had from that weekend road trip with your friends or your family trip to Italy. These experiences create close relationships, enrich your life, and become part of who you are. The uniqueness of your experiences makes them far more superior than material things. When you look back at your warmest memories, you won't remember your iPhone or Christmas presents, but rather the memory of the people you cared for and the time you shared with them.

It's the experience that counts.

Size Doesn't Matter

Most people believe that a large purchase equates to a large amount of happiness. But with happiness, size doesn't matter. In fact, it's the little things that count most.

Buying an expensive Ferrari may excite you more than dining out with your friends, but the thrill of that fancy car will eventually fade— especially if you have no one to drive to a fancy restaurant to share a special meal with you. Besides, with the money you spent on that vehicle, you could dine out in the company of friends and family for years. Those enjoyable evenings with loved ones will provide long-lasting, more fulfilling happiness that exceeds the temporary thrill of a large purchase.

Spending money on socializing such as dining out, going to a concert with friends, or meeting up for drinks is a great way to create lasting memories. Throw a party, take the day off, and do something amazing that you've never done before. Travel and take a vacation, preferably to a place that has more to offer than just sunbathing. Engage in new experiences from the local culture, cuisine, and music, and take in unique breath-taking views to create some of the most memorable moments in your life.

When you look back at your life in 30 years, what will your memories be? Except for those one-week annual vacations, will it be sitting behind your desk 365 days of the year? Or will it include… wine tasting in Tuscany, scuba diving in the Red Sea, snapping a selfie with the Pisa Tower, hiking in Tibet, a romantic weekend in Paris, seeing the sunrise at Angkor Wat, cheering your soccer team at the World Cup, sambaing until dawn in Rio, or sailing around the Mediterranean? That might be expensive for most and may not be feasible. But how about swimming with the dolphins, exploring a cave, skydiving, parasailing, scuba diving, feeding the sharks, riding in a hot air balloon, kite surfing, getting a tattoo, riding an elephant, driving a race car, seeing a volcano's mouth, hiking on a new trail, tubing down a river, witnessing a solar eclipse, meeting someone famous, exploring a rain forest, sending a message in a bottle, visiting a Buddhist temple, or walking on a glacier? These are far more accessible and equally exciting.

The World is *Your* Oyster

The world and what it has to offer is too vast for anyone to discover it completely. You better start exploring it while you're healthy and still able to enjoy it. Whether it is traveling, pampering yourself with a special treatment at the spa, or enjoying a nice dinner with a loved one, such experiences will enrich your life and stretch it in your mind.

Money is made to be spent, food is meant to be eaten, wine is meant to be drunk, and life is meant to be lived to the fullest. **You need to feel alive today and remind yourself why it's so great to be alive.**

Life isn't measured by your possessions or the dollar savings in your bank account, but by the amount of experiences you enjoyed in your life and the number of non-zero days you accumulated along the way.

Life's too short, so seize the day and enjoy it.

Fill Up the Bucket

The world is full of sensations waiting to be become memorable reminiscences, marvelous encounters waiting to be experienced, and spectacular wonders waiting to be observed. "On earth there is no heaven, but there are pieces of it everywhere," wrote Jules Renard.

You've been given an exclusive VIP invitation—a privilege denied to many—to spend a limited amount of time on this beautiful planet, so you'd better make the most of it. You can figure out what you want to do through compiling a whole-life bucket list.

A "Bucket List" is a great way to decide where to spend your precious time and money on generating novelty, creating experiences and memorable moments. It should comprise a list of approximately one hundred things you want to do before you die— things that can be very different and unique from one another. A bucket list is meant to be individual, unique, and incredibly personal.

Whole-Life Bucket Lists

Your whole-life bucket list should contain amazing things *you* would like to accomplish during this lifetime, regardless of when you'll have the chance to do them. Once you have the list, it will serve as a reminder that pushes you to make some time for the things that count.

Happily, you're never too young or too old to start this kind of list. But if you don't have a whole-life bucket list yet, make one fast; seeking happiness and doing something worthy with your time should start as early as possible in your life, because it will take some time to accomplish everything you write down.

As you fill this bucket list, be sure that it holds:

- the things you want to achieve in life
- the places you want to visit
- the things you want to see, the experiences you want to create with your loved ones
- anything that will make you feel fulfilled and happy.

Here is some helpful advice for brainstorming bucket-list items:

- **Dream big; the sky is the limit—within reason, of course.** Big dreams are great to include, but still make sure that they are somewhat realistic and achievable. By this I mean, a journey to outer space, no matter how fascinating or thrilling it may be, is not likely possible for you.

- **Dream small—include things that may seem ordinary and simple to achieve.** A bucket list is not about always doing things that are incredible or outstanding but *doing those things that make you happy and brighten your life.* Mix up your small goals with big ones; don't just write those goals that are harder to achieve. You want to write down smaller and simpler goals because having a sense of accomplishment, no matter how small, will definitely make you feel better and boost your self-confidence about getting to some of the items on your list.

- **Research and read about countries or sites that interest you, then plan to travel there.** Want to cross the Amazon River, spend Valentine's Day in Venice and New Year's in Dubai, dive in the Indian Ocean with the great white sharks, camp at Wadi Rum in Jordan, ski in Lebanon, attend an opera in Vienna, learn pizza-making in Napoli, or climb the world's highest peaks? There is so much to explore, even if you travel within your own country. As St. Augustine once said, "The world is a book, and those who don't travel only read one page."

- **Include things that are people-centric, not just ego-centric.** Usually most people will start with writing down goals that are rather ego-centric. It is far better to consider goals that involve other people as well. While we are tempted to think that actions involving ourselves will make us happy, the truth is that connecting with others actually brings about the happiest moments in our lives. So, instead of choosing to spend a day at the spa on your own, you may want to consider enjoying a trip with your family. The spa experience has a limited effect that disappears the next day but the family trip will have a positive impact on the relationship you have with the people you love that will last a long time.

- **Choose things you want to do this year, as well as sometime in the next ten years.**

Once you've put a whole-life bucket list together, read through it. Anything on your whole-life bucket list needs to satisfy just one question: **"If I knew that today was the last day of my life, would I really spend it doing this thing?"** If you answer "no" to a particular item, then you probably need to change it and replace it with something that has greater importance to you.

Having a whole-life bucket list is a great way to break away from the daily routine and force you to live and enjoy life. If you're running on a hamster wheel—stuck in hectic everyday schedules, to-do lists, and chores—you won't find the time to focus on the things that really matter unless you push yourself to create a bucket list.

Make it Manageable and Accessible

One hundred items seems like a lot, right? Let's make it a bit less daunting by breaking down your whole-life bucket list into weekly, monthly, yearly, and whole-life lists.

How do you decide what fills each? Consider the item's degree of importance to you, and its ease of achievement:

- **Weekly bucket lists contain things you'd like to do immediately.** Plan your week ahead with something enjoyable so it won't pass in vain. This could be a professional body massage, go a week without makeup, get a tattoo, ride in a canoe, or take a tennis lesson.

- **Monthly bucket lists contain things that take a bit more time to accomplish,** like creating your own personal recipe book, doing 20 random acts of kindness, or raising an ant farm.

- **Yearly bucket lists contain larger goals that have a deep significance for you,** like observing the Northern Lights at the North Pole, learning to play a musical instrument, or visiting the Pyramids in Egypt.

- **Life-long bucket list contains the things you will only do once in your lifetime**, like having children of your own, building your own home, or get a PHD in viticulture and enology!

Now that you've categorized your bucket items into certain time frames, you need to be sure to put your list in a place where you'll see it every day.

Think about where and when you spend your time in your home. Do you want to see it first thing in the morning? If so, do you want your bucket list to hang on the back of your bathroom door, or beside the bathroom mirror? Do you want to see the items and priorities for you each evening? If so, is it a good idea to hang it on a bulletin board in your kitchen while you prepare your dinner or dine? Or, is it the last thing you want to see at night, so you can dream about it? If so, place it on the end table by your bed.

Putting your bucket list in a place where you'll see it every day is the first step toward the actualization of your goals.

Actualizing Your Dreams and Goals

Once you've written down your bucket list, dedicate an hour or two each week to plan and work on your bucket list. The aim is **to eliminate something off your list each week, month, and year.**

Choose a goal from each of the bucket lists and think about what you need to do to make it happen. For example, if touring the pyramids of Egypt is on your list, start looking for information concerning taking such a trip. See how much a plane ticket will cost with accommodations, and so on. Take concrete steps toward its implementation. *Don't play the* "When I, then I'll" *game*; you'll just be leaving things until a later date and that date will keep getting pushed until you can no longer engage in it.

Musician John Lennon once wrote, "Life is what happens while we're busy making other plans." If your bucket list experiences remain as plans to be done "in the future," life will just happen, the years will march by, and valuable opportunities will be lost.

Evolving and Modifying

There will be times when you'll have to modify your bucket list if some of your goals do not longer fit your future vision.

A bucket list is not perfect, nor is it set in stone. You'll have to update it every once in a while, especially as things change in your life: you get married or divorced; you have a baby; you move to a different part of the country.

As you revise and update your bucket list, remember that it's your life and your happiness that's at stake here. **Your bucket list will help you take the steering wheel of your life and experience exciting things for**

a great and more fulfilling life. Do not wait until it is too late to do so. The purpose of life is to live it to the fullest. Go ahead and write your own life story.

Time Miracle Task

Start writing your bucket list now!

If you have children, get them to write their own bucket list.

If you have a partner, write a bucket list together.

<u>Weekly Bucket List:</u>

1. _____

2. _____

3. _____

4. _____

5. _____

<u>Monthly Bucket List:</u>

1. _____

2. _____

3. _____

4. _____

5. _____

Yearly Bucket List:

1. _____
2. _____
3. _____
4. _____
5. _____

Life-Long Bucket List:

1. _____
2. _____
3. _____
4. _____
5. _____

19

Investing in Yourself

Excellence for Life

∽

"The best moments in our lives are not the passive, receptive,
relaxing times. The best moments usually occur when our minds
are stretched to their limits in a voluntary effort to accomplish
something difficult and worthwhile."
– Mihaly Csíkszentmihályi

"Anyone who isn't embarrassed by who they were last year
probably isn't learning enough."
– Alain de Botton

The Best Interest

Research has shown that the activities that produce the most fulfillment
and enjoyment are those that are performed in a mental state known
as "flow"—also known as "in the zone." We talked about flow in Chapter
13. As a reminder, flow is a state of mind in which you are fully immersed
in a feeling of energized focus, full involvement, and complete absorption
in what you are doing to the extent you lose sense of space and time.

Flow generally occurs in active leisure, when people are doing their
favorite activities—gardening, cooking, painting, gaming, listening to

music, reading, playing a musical instrument, playing sports games, or socializing. These types of activities have the potential to produce a great number of memorable moments. Very rarely do people experience flow in passive leisure activities, such as watching television or relaxing on the couch.

Yet most people prefer to spend more of their free time staring at a screen of some kind than doing sports or performing their hobbies. Why is that? Why do people spend more of their free time doing something that has little chance of making them feel good?

Well, an activity that puts you "in the zone" normally requires an initial investment in yourself—some effort or training, for example—before it begins to be entertaining.

If you play the piano, for instance, you might recall that before you actually started enjoying this flow-inducing activity, you had to endure at least an hour of tedious practice every day. If you are a good tennis player who often gets into the "zone" while playing, you might be able to remember the long hours you had to spend practicing to reach the level you are at now. It takes some effort to become a musician, athlete, explorer, inventor, or artist who can spend time in a state of flow.

So, if you lack the dedication and discipline to surmount the initial hurdle of getting "good" at an entertaining activity or skill, you will likely settle for something that, like watching TV, is less enjoyable but more accessible. But every second you invest in honing a flow-inducing skill goes a long way to making your free time pursuits more gratifying and pleasant.

Investing in developing your skills and talents allows you to immerse in flow experiences that make for **excellence in life.** As Benjamin Franklin once wrote, "an investment in knowledge pays the best interest."

It really doesn't matter whether you learn a new skill, hone an existing one, develop yourself personally or professionally, or tap into your creativity; **when you invest your time in learning, you enrich your life and that of the people around you.** You grow in self-confidence and can help others by sharing what you learned and adding value to their lives.

Investing in yourself is all about growth. Who you were yesterday doesn't matter. What matters is whether you are growing right now and who you are going to be tomorrow. It's one of the best ways to spend your Life Essence—and it'll pay off dividends for the rest of your life.

Never Stop Learning

If you were to read the biographies of the top hundred most successful people in the world, you will find one common secret to their success: they all find time to step away from their work, slow down, and invest in activities that have a long-term payoff in knowledge and creativity. These are the small investments in learning that yield surprisingly large returns over time.

Some people have it in their character to enjoy learning, absorb new information, and experience the world to the fullest. For these individuals, life is long and rich.

Other people do not bother to learn anything new and are content to go with just the bare minimum. These people come to find that life will pass them by.

Ordinary people seek entertainment; extraordinary people seek learning. Evolutionary biologist Richard Dawkins puts it nicely:

After sleeping through a hundred million centuries we have finally opened our eyes on a sumptuous planet, sparkling with color, bountiful with life. Within decades we must close our eyes again. Isn't it a noble, an enlightened way of spending our brief time in the sun, to work at understanding the universe and how we have come to wake up in it?

Investing in professional knowledge and skills can take many forms. You can advance your education, take extra classes, enroll in workshops, attend conferences, or participate in webinars. You can expand your knowledge by reading books and articles. You can keep current on the latest trends or achievements by subscribing to publications or following expert blogs. These will contribute to your professional growth and boost your career by increasing your value to your employer. Your earning potential is likely to increase as you become a valuable asset deserving increased responsibilities and compensation. And… the more valuable you are, the more money you can make.

By earning more in less time, you will be able to spend the extra money on creating memories that stretch time in your mind. You will be able to retire early. **Investing in yourself is therefore investing in *your future.***

Or, you can invest in non-professional education, like learning to play a musical instrument. You can visit a museum, read a do-it-yourself book, take an art class, or start a new hobby. You can check the latest news in science and become a knowledge junkie. Learning a second language—or third—also has tremendous advantages; you will be able to experience a new culture and enjoy your travels more.

Besides, being fluent in more than one language will make you a more interesting person. Additionally, being bilingual has the potential for earning you more money as you become more valuable to your employer. Research[31] has also shown that learning a new language is one of the best brain workouts for preventing Alzheimer's and dementia.

Live a Thousand Lives

The most powerful, and low-cost way to learn is through Bill Gates's favorite learning medium: books.

The world's most successful people read at least one book per week. They are constantly learning. Theodore Roosevelt read one book a day when busy, and two to three a day when he had a free evening. Billionaire investor David Rubenstein reads six books a week, philanthropist and producer Oprah Winfrey credits reading for much of her success, business magnate Elon Musk read two books a day when he was younger, Facebook co-founder Mark Zuckerberg reads a book every two weeks, and Walt Disney Company CEO Bob Iger gets up every morning at 4:30 a.m. to read. Despite being responsible for running companies with more than a hundred thousand employees, multi-millionaire investor Warren Buffet estimates that he has spent 80 percent of his career reading and thinking.

Pick up a book! If you are not used to reading, it might take you some time to concentrate for long periods. Reading actually requires a bit of practice; you can't sit for an hour or two reading if you don't read often. It's an ability that develops over time. And with Kindle, eReaders, and audiobooks, finding an opportunity to read is easier than ever. If you drive or commute fifteen to thirty minutes to work each day, you can easily use that time to finish one audiobook each week.

You can also listen to a book while exercising. In the long run, you will have read hundreds of books and gained valuable knowledge on several topics. Find a topic that interests you and read a few related books before moving into a new topic. You will be able to learn something new every day.

Books contain someone's knowledge—in many cases, gathered over a lifetime—and compressed into a few pages that can be read in just a few hours. They provide the ultimate return on investment.

Reading is a powerful form of living because it creates memories that stick with you for a long time. If it's a self-help book, it will help you develop interesting skills. When you read you don't just learn new things; you live a thousand lives.

When you are absorbed in a book, you leave the borders of your reality for a little while and step into the mind of another person, perhaps in another age and culture. You experience the courage of a hero, the passion of a lover, and the sorrow of a bereaved. When you return back to yourself, you are never the same; you are enriched or inspired by living in that story.

When you look back at your life's memorable moments, you may find, a fascinating story from an amazing book that is as memorable for you as an adventure you actually took several years back. Both being significant experiences, you wouldn't be able to tell which had more weight in shaping your personality and leaving a trace in your mind. Your actual memories are just like the stories you find in books. The "remembering self" edits your actual experiences by erasing the dull parts, amplifying the pleasant parts, adding a dash of drama, and archiving the whole thing as a story in your mind. Every time you recall that story, it is edited until you become the hero of adventures that exists only in your mind, just like the stories that exist in books. By reading and collecting book memories, you enrich your own life and, as author C. S. Lewis wrote, "…in reading great literature I become a thousand men and yet remain myself."

Get Creative

Another way to invest in yourself is to explore your creative side. Each one of us has a fountain of creativity that needs to be unearthed. By engaging in creative activities, you develop certain areas of your brain that are critical to your personal development and the way you view problems and solutions. Here's what you can do instead of watching TV:

- sign up for an art class
- redecorate a room in your home
- try gourmet cooking
- start a hobby—perhaps gardening, bird watching, landscape photography, painting, or making pottery or jewelry. (As for me, I compose soundtrack music for films and write books.)

Whatever it is, use your untapped creativity to enrich your life.

Push Beyond

Challenge yourself and deliberately do things that *push your limits*. Long-term success comes from personal growth—and that can only occur when you push yourself beyond your comfort zone and start breaking your own records.

A fear of discomfort is often what's keeping you from living your best life. Albert Einstein wrote, "One should not pursue goals that are easily achieved. One must develop an instinct for what one can just barely achieve through one's greatest efforts."

No one ever came to this planet to take a back seat or play a secondary role. So find time to challenge yourself and grow your skills. Aim for small consistent change that'll make a big difference in the long run. You just need to be intent, to observe, to be willing to inquire, and to be open to learning. Life is short. Start being your best self, right now.

When you invest in yourself, do not fall into the trap of trying to improve your weaknesses. Your mind may be already conditioned to believe that if you suck at something, you need to spend time working on it and getting better. So instead of spending time getting better at what you are good at, you spend time to improve your weak areas.

Let's say on a scale of one to ten, you are a two at something. After spending precious time, effort, and energy, you might become a four at it. What's the real benefit? You are still below average—and you won't reap any substantial rewards from that.

You'll be more successful—and fulfilled—*if you are great at something and work harder to become even greater at it.*

If you are a great salesperson, work harder to become an even better salesperson. People will pay you for what you are great at, not what you are average at.

If you are an extremely creative person but cannot handle the finances, then focus on improving your creativity and get someone else to help advise you on investments and money.

You might be good at painting, music, photography, filming, cooking, or any other hobby, but have never given it time to develop fully. You can be great at those hobbies by enhancing your skills—through reading books, practicing the skill or talent, and attending courses.

Find out what you are good at, and become great at it.

Discover your uniqueness, and develop it.

Start investing in yourself now and enjoy a life full of success. It's never too late. As the Chinese proverb says, "The best time to plant a tree was 20 years ago. The second best time is now."

Time Miracle Task

Write down a list of skills and talents you are great at.

1. _____

2. _____

3. _____

4. _____

5. _____

Make a commitment to invest in yourself and list the ways you can improve those skills.

1. _____

2. _____

3. _____

4. _____

5. _____

20

Live The Moment

Savor!

∞

"Life moves pretty fast. If you don't stop and look around once
in a while, you could miss it."
– Ferris Bueller's Day Off

"If I were to begin life again, I should want it as it was. I would
only open my eyes a little more."
– Jules Renard

Living Each Moment

Life is a series of moments. It is not lived in daily or monthly
increments, but one moment at a time. Yet when we are planning
things, we tend to use somewhat large chunks of time: a dinner party
that will last four hours, a two-day weekend, a three-month school term,
a one-year lease, and so forth.

To expand our experience of time, we should try to live with **the
smallest interval of time possible in our minds**—say, one minute at a
time. When we become aware that life is lived at that time scale, we will
consciously make an effort to focus on the present and make the most of
each moment.

The time when we are fully alert of the present moments occurs mostly by pure chance. It could be a car crash, a glance from a stunning woman (or man), a shooting star, a sunset or a sunrise. Sometimes it is planned, such as the birth of a newborn baby. Whatever it is that captures our full attention, it makes our eyes open wide; it leaves us speechless. In those rare moments, we become fully alert, **and time slows down as our brains start recording every bit of detail from that event.**

When we recall that dense amount of information later, it will seem to us as if it was collected over a longer period of time. That's the reason why life-threatening events—car accidents, hurricanes, robberies—appear to go in slow motion, as if time has slowed down. This is due to a boost in our information-processing speed by our highly alert brain.

Fortunately we do not have to wait for such special (or tragic) events to occur by chance in order to slow the speed of time. **By focusing on the present moment, we can achieve a similar alertness level that will allow us to capture what is going on around us in more detail.**

By living in the present, we channel all our energy on what we are doing now, or on whom we are with. Living in the moment is all about being fully alive *now*. It occurs when you take a step back, meditate on some deep thoughts, take a deep breath, and smell some roses.

It occurs when you are mindful and fully immersed in what you are doing to the extent that you become totally oblivious to the passage of time.

By simply focusing on the present, your brain will absorb many more memories that otherwise would have gone unnoticed. Psychologists call this "savoring." In one study, participants who took a few minutes each day to savor something they usually rush through, such as eating a meal or having a cup of coffee, started experiencing more happiness and less depression in their lives.

So how do we learn to live in the present and savor the moment? It's not so difficult.

How to Savor the Moment

When on vacation, savor the tiny details unfolding around you, whether they involve eating a delicious dessert, enjoying the scenery, basking in the warm sunshine, or just feeling a gentle breeze off the ocean. This will create memorable moments that will stretch that holiday time in your mind, and allow you to recall it years later.

Plan your calendar using odd times. For example, set your alarm clock to wake you up at 6:23 a.m. instead of the usual 6:30. Have your reminder to go to the gym go off at 8:48 a.m. instead of 9:00. When you plan a meeting at work that starts at 10:30, put 10:26 a.m. in your calendar, so you not only make it on time, but also you break away from the common thirty- or sixty-minute view. That will help you focus and retain the individual moments that make up your day.

To enjoy the present, stop living in the past. You live in the moment when you stop living in the past, enjoy the present, and look forward to the future. Dwelling on the intrusive memories of the past—the things we should have done or not done, or things we should have said or not said—is an immense and useless drain of brainpower. Negative thinking makes us unhappy, whereas living in the present can make us happier.

Refrain from worrying about the future—it does not help. Novelist Paulo Coelho notes, "We think so much about the future that we neglect the present, and thus experience neither the present nor the future." When we are at work, we dream about being on vacation, and when on vacation, we worry about all the work that is stacking up for our return. Our brain's default mode of operation is future thinking, and so we all worry about things that might happen and anticipate future events. But most worries are exaggerated scenarios that never happen. As humorist Mark Twain said, "I have known a great many troubles, but most of them never happened."

Practice a meditation technique called "mindfulness." As you read these words printed on this page, take in a deep breath. Focus on the rise of your abdomen on the in-breath, and the stream of heat through your nostrils—and become aware of being alive. By having that feeling right now, you'll be living in the moment.

This kind of meditation enhances the awareness of the present as it is unfolding now. It slows down time subjectively, creating the feeling that there is ample time to achieve the things we want to do. It is not that difficult, even for people who have never practiced meditation.

In one study[32], people who were trained to do it for just twenty minutes a day for five days showed a significant improvement in concentration skills and had lower anxiety and stress symptoms. Studies have also shown that mindfulness reduces stress, boosts the immune system, lowers blood pressure, and reduces the risk of heart disease.

Cure "the Rush"—Be Mindful

It's easy to get into a mindless routine at work and home where every moment becomes a race against the clock. You spend a typical day doing dull unchallenging tasks at work, then running your weekly errands and the standard family interactions in the evening. By the time you're ready for bed, you think, "Where did the day go?" When that occurs, you get the scary feeling that there is not enough time to do all the things you want to do.

In rushing through the day, you also don't remember things as vividly and the day is forgotten as if it never existed. It feels like you're racing through life instead of actually living it. *Mindfulness can be the cure to rush.*

Cultivating a focused awareness on the present moment through mindfulness meditation can make you more engaged and you actually perceive time as having slowed down. You'll have more control of your life and feel like you are using your time more wisely. This was observed in studies perfumed with Buddhist monks who experience expanding time durations when they close their eyes and focus on the present moment.

Mindfulness meditation can also teach us the kind of focus that brings more intensity to our experiences, thus making them more memorable. That focus also allows us to notice new things and experience life in a novel way. It will allow us to approach even the most mundane tasks in a spirit of exploration and curiosity and in so doing, deeply change our perception of those activities. This is great for collecting the necessary mental snapshots that our mind will later use to recreate the time spent on those activities, and eventually the perceived span of our life.

With enough practice, mindfulness can become an almost permanent mental state, often described as a "presence of mind" when we are clearly aware of our inner and outer world, including our thoughts, sensations, and emotions as they occur at any given moment.

By being mindful of the present, life will not be allowed to pass by without living it. Life unfolds in the present, so we should seize that precious moment and absorb its peculiarities before they slip away unobserved.

Stop and look at that weird cloud in the sky or at that beautiful sunset. When having a meal, rather than reading the newspaper or checking the latest on social media, concentrate on the taste of the food. Savor at least the first three bites. Spend more time on those fleeting moments that bring meaning to life: reading to your children, chatting with your friend, having a glass of wine with your partner.

Just soak in as much of today as you possibly can— the sights, sounds, smells, and emotions—and when you look back at the time spent, it will feel much longer. It's a short journey, so make sure you are present to fully embrace the ride.

Time Miracle Task

Write a list of the main things you want to implement in your life from this book.

1. _____

2. _____

3. _____

4. _____

5. _____

6. _____

7. _____

8. _____

9. _____

10. _____

Epilogue

Watching Your Marvelous Life Movie

∞

We all strive to be wise in how we invest and spend our money. How much wiser we should be when it comes to spending our time, which is considerably more precious.

By understanding how you spend your limited time on basic needs, earning money, and enjoying life, and applying some of the hacks presented here, you can maximize your own "Life Essence" and appreciate the time miracle you've acquired even more. You would then be able to make the most of that scarce time and fill it with memorable moments that will last forever.

And when your time is up, and you look back at the life you have lived, it will be different.

Instead of feeling that you were 20 years old just yesterday, and wonder how the decades of your life passed in the blink of an eye, you can run the film of your endless precious memories in your mind, from your sensational adventures and the exciting places you visited, all the way through to the interesting people you met and all that knowledge you acquired along the way.

At that moment, instead of seeing your life flash before your eyes in a split second, you will be satisfied to watch it peacefully unfold… and take pleasure in the gratifying feeling of having been able to fit several lifetimes into a single one. And that is by far the ultimate Time Miracle!

THE END

Author's Note

⤳✦⤳

Enjoyed the Book? You can make a big difference.

Thank you for reading *The Time Miracle*. I hope you found it beneficial.

If you enjoyed the book and have a minute to spare, I would very grateful if you could post a review (as short as you like) on my book's Amazon page.
You can jump right to the page by clicking on the link below

Click Here to Post a Review on Amazon

https://www.amazon.com/product-reviews/B07FMD2WCQ/

Honest reviews from readers like you make a massive difference in spreading the message and helping new readers **appreciate how precious our time is and ways to make the most of it.**

You can also check my other book *The Power of Time Perception* to learn why time speeds up as we grow older and ways to slow it down.
https://www.amazon.com/dp/B01MZEZL7S

Thank you so much!
Jean Paul

P.S. If you'd like to know when my next book comes out and want to receive occasional updates from me, then sign up for my newsletter here -> http://www.jpzogby.com

Without Whom

ⷜ∕∕◌

I know that I wouldn't accomplish a fraction of the things I want to do if it wasn't for my awesome family and friends. So, a special thanks to Roula, Stephanie, Chloe, and Anthony—the best family ever—for their endless love, support, and patience.

I owe a great deal of gratitude to my Editors, Elizabeth Zack, Beth Dorward, and Anna Hogarty, for their valuable role in shaping the final book. Elizabeth and Beth, I admire the way you challenge my logic and your sharp eye to detail was instrumental. Anna, your suggestions were invaluable.

I would also like to thank Andrej Semnitz for designing a stunning and awesome book cover. Thank you for bearing with me in all those endless changes I kept requesting.

Without the psychologists, and various academics who spent years performing studies and conducting experiments, this book would not have been possible. Thank you for your relentless efforts.

Last but not least, I think all my readers and followers who read my first book and encouraged me to write this second one. Thank you for spreading the awareness about "time," our most precious resource.

References

1. Kean, S. *The Violinist's Thumb*. (2013).
2. Burn-Callander, R. UK workers waste a year of their lives in useless meetings. *Management Today* (2013).
3. Moderate exercise: No pain, big gains. *Harv. Mens. Health Watch* (2007). at <https://www.health.harvard.edu/newsletter_article/Moderate_exercise_No_pain_big_gains>
4. Bilgin, B. & LeBoeuf, R. A. Looming Losses in Future Time Perception. *Journal of Marketing Research* **47**, 520–530 (2010).
5. Kripke DF1, Garfinkel L, Wingard DL, Klauber MR, M. M. Mortality associated with sleep duration and insomnia. *Arch Gen Psychiatry.* **59(2):131-**, (2002).
6. Gardner, J. & Oswald, A. J. Money and mental wellbeing: A longitudinal study of medium-sized lottery wins. *J. Health Econ.* **26**, 49–60 (2007).
7. Foundation, N. S. How Much Sleep Do We Really Need? *Sleep* at <https://sleepfoundation.org/excessivesleepiness/content/how-much-sleep-do-we-really-need-0>
8. Modern Hunter–Gatherers Probably Get Less Sleep Than You Do. *Sci. Am.* (2015). at <https://www.scientificamerican.com/article/modern-hunter-gatherers-probably-get-less-sleep-than-you-do/>
9. Crous-Bou, M. *et al.* Mediterranean diet and telomere length in Nurses' Health Study: population based cohort study. *BMJ* **349**, g6674 (2014).

10. Hurst, Y. & Fukuda, H. Effects of changes in eating speed on obesity in patients with diabetes: a secondary analysis of longitudinal health check-up data. *BMJ Open* **8,** e019589 (2018).

11. Balancing paid work, unpaid work and leisure. *OECD* (2018). at <http://www.oecd.org/gender/balancing-paid-work-unpaid-work-and-leisure.htm>

12. Ekelund, U. *et al.* Physical activity and all-cause mortality across levels of overall and abdominal adiposity in European men and women: the European Prospective Investigation into Cancer and Nutrition Study (EPIC). *Am. J. Clin. Nutr.* **101,** 613–621 (2015).

13. Cermakova, P. *et al.* Living Alone with Alzheimer's Disease: Data from SveDem, the Swedish Dementia Registry. *J. Alzheimers. Dis.* **58,** 1265–1272 (2017).

14. Yoshitake, T. *et al.* Incidence and risk factors of vascular dementia and Alzheimer's disease in a defined elderly Japanese population: the Hisayama Study. *Neurology* **45,** 1161–8 (1995).

15. Nielsen. The average American watches so much TV it's almost a full-time job. *Buisness Insider* (2016). at <http://www.businessinsider.com/how-much-tv-do-americans-watch-2016-6>

16. Evan Assano. How Much Time Do People Spend on Social Media? (2017). at <https://www.socialmediatoday.com/marketing/how-much-time-do-people-spend-social-media-infographic>

17. Howard, J. Americans devote more than 10 hours a day to screen time, and growing. (2016). at <https://edition.cnn.com/2016/06/30/health/americans-screen-time-nielsen/index.html>

18. Beckford, M. Every hour of TV watching shortens life by 22 minutes. (2011). at <https://www.telegraph.co.uk/news/health/

news/8702101/Every-hour-of-TV-watching-shortens-life-by-22-minutes.html>

19. Prolonged television viewing linked to increased risk of type 2 diabetes, cardiovascular disease, and premature death. *Harvard Sch. Public Heal.* (2011). at <https://www.hsph.harvard.edu/news/press-releases/tv-diabetes-cardiovascular-disease-premature-death/>

20. Dr. David Snowden. The Nun Study. (1986). at <https://www.psychiatry.umn.edu/research/research-labs-and-programs/nun-study>

21. James Banks, J. N. and A. S. *The dynamics of ageing: Evidence from the English Longitudinal Study of Ageing 2002-12 (Wave 6).* (2014).

22. Brickman, Philip Coates, Dan Janoff-Bulman, R. Lottery winners and accident victims: Is happiness relative? *J. Pers. Soc. Psychol.* **36,** 917–927 (1978).

23. Buettner, D. *The Blue Zones Solution.* (2017).

24. Wilson, E. Want to live to be 100? *The Guardian* (2001).

25. Sone, T. *et al.* Sense of Life Worth Living (Ikigai) and Mortality in Japan: Ohsaki Study. *Psychosom. Med.* **70,** 709–715 (2008).

26. Olds, James Milner, P. Positive reinforcement produced by electrical stimulation of septal area and other regions of rat brain. *J. Comp. Physiol. Psychol.* **47,** 419–427 (1954).

27. Van Boven, L. & Ashworth, L. Looking forward, looking back: anticipation is more evocative than retrospection. *J. Exp. Psychol. Gen.* **136,** 289–300 (2007).

28. Nawijn, J., Marchand, M. A., Veenhoven, R. & Vingerhoets, A. J. Vacationers Happier, but Most not Happier After a Holiday. *Appl. Res. Qual. Life* **5,** 35–47 (2010).

29. Tali Sharot. *The Optimism Bias: A Tour of the Irrationally Positive Brain*. (Pantheon, 2011). at <http://www.amazon.com/The-Optimism-Bias-Irrationally-Positive/dp/B00D1GCC5Q>

30. Pchelin, P. & Howell, R. T. The hidden cost of value-seeking: People do not accurately forecast the economic benefits of experiential purchases. *J. Posit. Psychol.* **9,** 322–334 (2014).

31. Moskowitz, C. Learning a Second Language Protects Against Alzheimer's. *Live Sci.* (2011). at <https://www.livescience.com/12917-learning-language-bilingual-protects-alzheimers.html>

32. Tang, Y.-Y. *et al.* Short-term meditation training improves attention and self-regulation. *Proc. Natl. Acad. Sci. U. S. A.* **104,** 17152–6 (2007).

About the Author

❦

Jean Paul Zogby, author of *The Time Miracle* and *The Power of Time Perception* is a writer, researcher, music composer, and real estate development expert.

His current passion is to help people appreciate how valuable time is, why time appears to speed up as we grow older, and how to make the most of it. With the last six years spent researching time perception in the fields of Neuroscience and Cognitive Psychology, he is passionate about sharing what science has to say about our experience of time.

In his free time, Jean Paul composes soundtrack music for film and also publishes research in Astrophysics related to the formation of planetary solar systems.

A husband and father of two lovely daughters and a son, he resides in Dubai where he is the CEO on a multi-billion-dollar construction project.

For more details on Zogby's life and publications, and to subscribe to his mailing list, visit this official website:

http://www.jpzogby.com

There, you can download a free copy of *Healthy Brain Diet* and take the online Speed of Time Test to measure how fast time runs in your mind.

Made in the USA
San Bernardino, CA
02 June 2019